Worthy
See Yourself as God Does

Amanda Mortus

Worthy
See Yourself as God Does

Copyright © 2013, Amanda Mortus. All rights reserved.

No part of this publication may be reproduced, stored in a retrieval system, or transmitted in any form or by any means – electronic, mechanical, photocopy, recording, or any other – except for brief quotations in printed reviews, without the prior permission of the author.

Mortus, Amanda
Worthy: see yourself as God does / Amanda Mortus
ISBN: 978-1482747560

Unless otherwise noted, Scripture passages have been taken from the *New American Bible with Revised New Testament and Revised Psalms*. Copyright 1991, 1986, 1970 by the Confraternity of Christian Doctrine (CCD), Washington, D.C.. All rights reserved. Quotes are taken from the English translation of the *Catechism of the Catholic Church* for the United States of America (indicated as *CCC*), 2nd ed. Copyright 1997 by United States Conference – Liberia Editrice Vaticana.

Cover and interior design by Amanda Mortus
Cover images © Amanda Mortus
Author photo © Myra Wilson Photography

To Mary, the perfect example of womanhood,
and to Jesus, who finds me worthy,
even when I feel like I'm not.

Kathy,
May God dwell richly in your heart and always fill you with His love and peace!
In Christ,
Amanda ♡

Contents

Introduction
Section One: The Lies

Relational _____ 7

Unseen _____ 20

Unsought _____ 33

Unpursued _____ 43

Unworthy _____ 57

Section Two: The Triumph of Love

Help Me… _____ 73

Monkey Bars _____ 87

Eve and Mary _____ 100

Seen, Sought, Pursued, Worthy _____ 114

The Proposal That Never Ends _____ 130

Section Three: The Truth and the Challenge

Invitation _____ 145

Precious Little _____ 158

Strength _____ 172

Dignity _____ 194

Laughter _____ 206

Fierce _____ 223

Acknowledgments

Introduction

"Try to learn what is pleasing to the Lord. Take no part in the fruitless works of darkness; rather expose them, for it is shameful even to mention the things done by them in secret; but everything exposed by the light becomes visible, for everything that becomes visible is light. Therefore, it says: 'Awake, O sleeper, and arise from the dead, and Christ will give you light.'" – Ephesians 5:10-14

In attempting to write this introduction, the pressure for that first word, that glorious first sentence, overwhelmed me. In all honesty, I seriously considered writing the whole book and then writing the introduction last, because the beginning seemed so daunting. I wondered, "Where would I begin? What could I possibly say that would hook a reader and entice them to continue reading?" The answer that kept coming was: "Nothing. Nothing." I kept thinking and believing that there was nothing I could say that would hook you. Not a single thing. At first that answer may sound hopeless, but when you look deeper, it is in fact filled with hope.

While there may be nothing that I could say to hook you, there is an infinite amount that God has to say that will hook you, intrigue you, and invite you to go deeper. In fact, I hope that He speaks far more through this book than I shall, for I am but a happy scribe of the Most High (it is important to note that, by the grace of God, I am quite different from the Scribes Jesus so often chastised). So it is that I let Him begin this book, through the words He inspired Saint Paul to write so many years ago. In many ways, that verse says it all, and the first word is the only hook I need. *Try.* We are imperfect beings, but we are called to keep trying. In my Theology 101 class Father Chris Kirchgessner, O.S.B. taught that we don't sin because we are human, we sin because we are being less than we were created to be. It is a thought, a truth that has resonated with me ever since those early discussions in my first theology class. Our humanity is not what is holding us back. We like to blame our humanity, our fallen nature; we like to blame Adam and Eve because it is easier to blame someone else rather than take responsibility for being less than we were created to be. Yes, we will sin – we read in Matthew's gospel that the spirit is willing, but the flesh is weak – but we must keep striving to learn what is pleasing to the Lord.

While you will get snapshots of me throughout this book, it is my hope that you see more of God and less of me. As John the Baptist said, "He must increase; I must decrease" (John 3:30). May the darkness in your life be dispelled, and the lies that you have been told exposed. Perhaps you feel alive; perhaps you feel as though you already are who you were created to be. Perhaps not. Perhaps you feel dead, confused about who you are, *whose* you are and who you were created to be. Maybe you are somewhere in the middle, just beginning to figure out your purpose in life, but unsure how to get there. No matter where your heart lies in that spectrum, I pray that you will find hope and light in this book. May this book call you to come back from the dead and awaken your heart; may it shine the light of Christ in the darkest depths of your heart. It is my prayer that this book touches you more deeply than He has touched me, and if, in fact, that happens, then all the struggle will be worth it, both His and mine (which is eternally smaller in comparison). He has spoken to and continues to speak to my heart. He shines His light on all of us; may this book shine from His heart to mine and to yours.

As I began to plot out my dreams for this book, I prayed about what to write and what to convey. As I sat down to actually write the book, I came across that verse from Ephesians. The more I read it the more perfect it is for the journey we are about to embark upon, both in reading this book and in our lives. If you flip through the chapters you'll find what I hope to be the embodiment of Saint Paul's words. Throughout this book we will try to learn what is pleasing to the Lord, call out the lies and expose fruitless works, cling to the light and to what is visible, and hopefully, by the end of it all, arise from the dead and be awakened by the light and love of Christ. This journey of life is a long one, it started the day you were born and won't really end until you meet Jesus in Heaven. Or, perhaps, that is where the real quest truly begins. Either way you look at it, we are on a quest to find our own hearts, and hopefully we are journeying *towards* something, some One. So we embark, we set out on this road not knowing what we will find or what troubles may befall us, and we wait to see what awaits us just around the river bend. Hopefully this book can be a compass on the journey, pointing you on, encouraging you to be exactly what you were created to be: *worthy*.

The Lies

"Above all, don't lie to yourself. The man who lies to himself and listens to his own lie comes to a point that he cannot distinguish the truth within him, or around him, and so loses all respect for himself and for others. And having no respect he ceases to love."

– Fyodor Dostoevsky

Relational

"God created man in his image; in the divine image he create him; male and female he created them." – Genesis 1:27

We were made first and foremost in the image and likeness of God. In order to understand who we are as women, the best answer comes from the beginning, from our roots in our creation. We look to Scripture and find that we are created in His image and likeness. What does that mean? It means we are reflections of greatness, of majesty and of a beauty so magnificent, so glorious that we can never fully behold it in this life. Moses begged God to let him see His glory and the Lord responded, "But you cannot see my face, for no one can see me and live."[1] This story of Moses often reminds me of the song "Show Me Your Glory" by Third Day. Through this song we can relate to Moses, we just want to see and behold the God who created us. The band sings about catching a glimpse of God's splendor and how it is the most amazing thing they have ever seen. Seeing God's splendor, however tiny a glimpse they get, they know that they'll never be the same again. How amazing it would be to catch but a glimpse of His splendor, for we know we would never be the same, and so did Moses. The Lord allowed Moses to see not His face, but His back, and Moses spent forty days and nights with the Lord writing down the Ten Commandments on the stone tablets. Moses spent this time living the chorus that Third Day sings, humbly pleading with God that He would show us His glory, that He would reveal to us His face. We

---

[1] Exodus 33:20

long to see the majesty that shines all around Him because we know that we can't go on without God. God's majesty shone on Moses, and Moses believed and knew that He could not go on without Him. When Moses returned from Mount Sinai he had become so radiant that Aaron and the other Israelites "were afraid to come near him."[2] Because we were created in His image and likeness, we are reflections of Him who is more resplendent than we can bear to see and still live. We have a beauty within us, not so much because of who we are but because of *whose* we are. We are God's and His beauty shines within us, longing to be shared with the world.

God is relational to the core. He is so relational that He exists in Trinitarian form: Father, Son and Holy Spirit. He exists in the most perfect relationship we could ever imagine. We, particularly as women, embody this relational characteristic of God and are formed out of the Trinitarian relationship. All people are formed out of the Trinitarian relationship; all people were created for relationship with one another, and with God. We were not only made in the image and likeness of the Trinitarian relationship, we were made *for* relationship. Scripture tells us two accounts of the creation of humans. In the first account we learned that we are made in His image and likeness. In the second story of creation we learn more about why women were created: so that man would not be alone.

It is far too easy for many men and women to take the second story of creation the wrong way. Women were not made to follow men around like lost little puppies in need of a home. We

---

[2] cf. Exodus 33:21-34:30

were made as companions, helpers, confidants, friends, partners for men (we were also made to be friends and companions to other women, but more on that later). We were made so that man would not be alone, though I have no doubt that had woman been created first, man would have been created so that woman would not be alone. We were both created for each other so that neither one had to be alone. We need each other; we need friendship, companionship, and someone to commiserate with. So the first account of creation tells us about how man and woman are created in God's image, while the second account tells us, in greater detail, about the creation of woman:

> "The Lord God said: "It is not good for the man to be alone. I will make a suitable partner for him." The Lord God then built up into a woman the rib that he had taken from the man. When he brought her to the man, the man said: "This one, at last, is bone of my bones and flesh of my flesh; This one shall be called 'woman,' for out of 'her man' this one has been taken." The man and his wife were both naked, yet they felt no shame."[3]

In the second account of creation, we encounter the first time that God says that something in creation is *not* good. Everything up to this point that was created, God says that it is good. However, we read that it is *not* good that man should be alone, so God creates a partner fit for him.

When the woman was created Adam said, "This one, *at last*, is bone of my bones and flesh of my flesh." *At last.* God created everything else in the universe and said it was good. God

---

[3] Genesis 2: 18, 22-23, 25

created Adam, and Adam, himself a reflection of God, says, *at last*. She is the long awaited creation; she is the crown jewel, the prize, the final brushstroke of the masterpiece of creation. If creation were a great symphony, Eve would be the final, stunning crescendo. If creation were a magnificent fireworks display, then Eve takes her place in those final minutes where all the fireworks explode and light up the night sky, filling us with wonder and awe. The whole story of creation builds and builds, and each day God creates something more amazing than the last.

Why does dessert come at the end of a meal? Because we like to save the best for last. Why, when we go to a concert, do the big bands perform last? Because the big names are what we are waiting to see, and they are worth the wait. Why does each performer save their best songs for the encore? Because just when we think the concert is over, they come back out and wow us with their best song. God is the same way. We think creation is over, He has created Adam in His own image, how much better can it get? It seems that the concert of creation is over, God has said His goodbyes, thanked His adoring fan (remember it was only Adam alive at this point) and left the stage. Then He comes back out and gives us an encore we will never forget: He creates woman.

Imagine Adam in the Garden of Eden, hungry, longing for someone who is like him. He is lonely and he wakes from his slumber and the first thing that we hear out of his mouth isn't, "God what did you do with my rib?" but rather, "This one, *at last*, is bone of my bone and flesh of my flesh." His concern has nothing to do with himself, but instead, his concern, his excitement, his deep joy comes from finally having found one who is like him. She is not his exact identical, but she is like him, his equal, and he is no longer alone.

Think about the way the woman we will come to call Eve was created; she was created unlike any other. Every other human being is born of a woman; Eve is created out of the rib bone of a man. Don't you think that God was saying something special here? Perhaps it is strange to think about, but because Eve's creation is so different from the way *every other human* is born, it is reasonable to think that God was pointing to something special with her. After all, wasn't God pointing to something special when Jesus was born of a virgin? Why should Eve's unusual creation be any different? She was to be the crown of creation. She was special. She was made differently because she was made for a different purpose than Adam was. Adam was made "out of the clay of the ground."[4] Eve was made out of Adam's rib. Men tend to be more work-oriented. Their focus in life is their work, and on what they accomplish because they were made out of the foundation of God's work: the Earth. Women, on the other hand, tend to be more relationship-oriented. Their focus in life is on their family, their friends, their relationships, both friendships and romantic in nature, because they were made out of a person, out of a bone near the heart no less!

Still, there is more truth to be discovered about the heart of a woman in the second story of creation. The author of Genesis writes, "The man and his wife were both naked, yet they felt no shame."[5] If what you get out of that verse is that we weren't

---

[4] Genesis 2:7.

created to wear clothes then you are missing the point entirely. We, both men and women, were created *perfectly*. We didn't need the latest issue of Vogue magazine to tell us what to wear, how to do our hair, what make up would bring out our eyes the most, or what jeans would be the most flattering to our back-sides. We were created perfectly, just the way we were, in our naked, uninhibited, unhindered form. Because we were created perfectly, we felt no shame. We were not created to live in shame, or to be ashamed of ourselves. There is a difference between shame and humility. We were made for one, not the other. We often think that by shrinking, by down-playing who we are and the gifts we bear, we are being humble. We don't want to be proud beings and flaunt our talents about, lest others think we are arrogant. Instead, we shrink, we slouch, we hide, and over time we begin to believe that there isn't any good within us anymore. John Eldredge writes, "Shame says, 'I'm nothing to look at. I'm not capable of goodness.' Humility says, 'I bear a glory for sure, but it is a reflected glory. A grace given to me.' Your story does not begin with sin. It begins with a glory bestowed upon you by God. It does not start in Genesis 3; it starts in Genesis 1."[6] Shame is not the attitude or the frame of mind we were made for, it leads us to think that we are not capable of goodness, much less greatness. In fact, we were made for greatness, we were made for glory. We are reflections of the greatest glory ever to exist. We were not created to stand in front of a mirror and criticize our own thighs, hips, nose, ears, hair

---

[5] Genesis 2:25

[6] Eldredge, John. *Waking the Dead: The Glory of a Heart Fully Alive*. Nashville, TN: Thomas Nelson, 2003. 77.

color, arms, teeth, smile or anything. We were created in the image of the most beautiful God we shall ever know. When we stand in front of the mirror and criticize our own image, we criticize the image of the very God who created us, the God whose image we are made in. Who are we to criticize the most wondrous being in the entire universe? We were created free from shame. If only we had stayed that way, this story might have a different ending.

Oh, The Fall

Don't we all wish the story ended there? We all know what comes next: that darn tree, that darn serpent and The Fall. We wish we could just stop reading there, ignore the fact that there is a huge book waiting for us after the first ten or so pages. We would love to pretend that we lived happily ever after in the Garden of Eden, naked and free from shame. But we didn't. I say 'we' here because even though we as individuals weren't alive at the time of creation, we had a role in it and we are living in the results of The Fall. It was Adam and Eve that ate of the tree of knowledge, but given the option, we probably would have made the same decision. We too would have been prey to the cunning, twisted words of the serpent. We would have listened just as much, if not more so, than Adam and Eve did. After all, have we figured out how to be perfect people who only ever listen to God? Not yet. So, we listened to that little serpent, we ate of the tree we were forbidden to eat from and we allowed and convinced Adam to eat with us. God came around and suddenly we were filled with shame and we hid from Him. We wanted to clothe ourselves, cover ourselves from the love of God because deep down we knew we had disobeyed Him and we felt we were no longer worthy of His love, and it all unravels from there.

Remember how Eve's unusual creation meant that God was pointing to something special about her? Since God was pointing to something special about Eve, don't you think she also has a special role in explaining why things are the way they are in our own feminine hearts? If she is who we were created to be, if we are reflections of her as her daughters, then it makes sense that The Fall affects not only Eve, but every woman after her. See how quickly we can go from rooting for Eve, from praising her as the crown of creation to condemning her and blaming her for all of our faults? It is a quick downfall and we, especially as women, are so quick to blame and point the finger. The things we'd like to do or say to Eve if we could are as numerous as the stars in the sky, but we can't undo what has already happened. We can, however, learn from it.

We know that Eve must have been beautiful, she was, after all, the crown of creation, the cream of the crop, the last word of creation, the final crescendo of the symphony of creation. We know that she was created out of and for relationship. She was created so that together she and Adam could be fruitful and multiply. We know that she was loved intensely by God. It follows that because she was loved intensely and fiercely by God, that Satan intensely and fiercely hated her. All of the things God loved about Eve were all of the things that Satan hated most about her: her beauty, her relational heart, her desire for her husband. Even after The Fall God tells Eve, "yet your urge shall be for your husband, and he shall be your master"; Eve longs for Adam, her desire, her urge, the deepest pangs in her heart are for her husband.[7] Rest assured that all of the things Satan hates about Eve are the same things he hates about women today, and because of this, they are the very things Satan attacks first.

    Wouldn't you love to be like Eve before The Fall, to know that you were created by a God who loves you, and who dotes on you? To be like Even in the Garden of Eden, before Satan started his never-ending assault on humanity would be a dream. Life in the Garden sounds so simple, so carefree, and so easy. You wouldn't be filled with doubt or worry, you would simply be. You would be with your husband and you would be with God, with nothing in the way. Deep down, this is what we long for because that is what we were made for. It, in some way, is also what Satan was made for. If you'll remember, Satan wasn't always Satan. He was once an angel, the greatest of all the angels. He was the crown of the angels, if you will. He had it all and yet he wanted more. He wanted to rule Heaven, he wanted to be God's equal. So Satan fought God and he lost. Since he knows he can't win with God, his only hope is to win over God's prized creation, and bring her over to his side with lies and deceit, by playing with our hearts. Satan doesn't win Woman over because she is weak or inferior, he doesn't go after Woman because she is easily won over or stupid, nor does he go after Woman because she is alone for Genesis tells us that she was not.[8] These are some of the countless lies Satan uses against woman today, the lies that Satan leads us to hold in the depths of our hearts and souls.

---

[7] Genesis 3:16

[8] Genesis 3:6.

However, Woman is not weak or inferior, she is not easily won over, she is not stupid, and she is not alone. Satan goes after Woman because he knows that she is the crown of creation, just as he was once the crown of the angels. He goes after her because winning her over is the greatest victory he can hope for. Satan doesn't want the little prizes, the plants and the animals, he wants the biggest prize he can get his grubby little hands on: Woman.

Satan, before he rebelled, wanted the one thing he couldn't have: more power. He saw it and yet it eluded him, it was just out of his grasp. He must have felt he deserved it because he was God's favorite angel. He used that same poorly reasoned logic to get at Woman. Scripture tells us that the serpent says to the woman, "Did God *really* tell you not to eat from any of the trees in the garden?"[9] Can't you just hear the cunning trickery in the serpent's hissing voice? I imagine him a bit like Gollum in *The Lord of the Rings* movies, whispering creepily under his breath. Maybe the serpent is like the firefighters in those pin-up calendars with a soft and smooth, warm and inviting voice. Either way, he is a devious and tricky serpent. Eve tells the serpent that there is only one tree they are not allowed to eat from.[10] Satan already knew there was one thing that God told her she couldn't have so he made it seem elusive to Eve, he made her think she deserved it, after all, she was the crown of creation. Satan presses Eve, "You certainly will not die! No, God knows well that the moment you eat of it your eyes will be opened and you will be like gods

---

[9] Genesis 3:1, emphasis added.

[10] God explicitly tells Adam this before Woman's creation (see Genesis 2:16), though she clearly articulates God's command to the serpent.

who know what is good and what is bad."[11] Oh, he is a conniving and devious little devil. This verse points us to the Gospel according to John which says that "When he [Satan] tells a lie, he speaks in character, because he is a liar and the father of lies."[12] He lies to Eve and he continues to lie to us. He tells Eve that she will not die. He practically says, "How could you die? God wants your eyes to be open, eat, eat, eat. You will be like *gods*, you will be adored and revered, awesome and powerful." Satan purposely leaves out the fact that God already adores and loves Woman. The serpent tempts us with all the things that pride wants and we begin to doubt that we have it all in the Garden of Eden.

    The evil characters in the movies we watched as children can't help but come to our mind. They were modeled after him, the father of lies. Scar convinces Simba that he is responsible for the death of Mufasa. Ursula convinces Ariel to sell her voice so that she can become a human. The witch offers Snow White the poisoned apple, enticing her with its beauty and tastiness. Even in *Enchanted* as Pip tries to tell the story of Nathaniel's misdeeds to Prince Edward he mutters about the poisoned apple, "It's good!" If only it were as good as Satan, the witch and Nathaniel make the apple, the poisoned, forbidden fruit out to be. But that isn't the case. Satan is the father of lies and truth is not a word that exists in his vocabulary. He tempts, he twists, and he is cunning. The protagonists in the stories sell themselves short and end up with even less than they bargained for. The story is literally as old as time.

---

[11] Genesis 3:4-5.

[12] John 8:44.

Satan gets at the heart of Eve, "You will be more like God if you eat of that tree." Now she wants more, she forgets that she already has it all, and only sees that she *nearly* has it all. Nearly just isn't good enough for her, just as nearly wasn't good enough for Satan, and so she thinks that God must be holding out on her. Eve, as we all do, feels wronged. How dare they hold out on me? No matter whom "they" are, especially when it comes to God. Pride doesn't leave room for rationality, and pride has no real friends, it only sees what it doesn't have and what it believes it is rightfully due. Eve is aware of the fact that she is the Crown of Creation, and this knowledge makes room for pride to enter in. Woman eats from the tree, and so does Adam. We read the story and we shout at them, "Don't do it!" It is like watching your favorite sports team and yelling at the TV screen as if the players can actually hear you and will listen to your advice. It is like watching Scar trick Simba into believe Mufasa's death is his fault. It is like watching Ariel sell her voice and yelling at her not to. It is like watching *Snow White* and hoping, praying that she doesn't eat the apple. Every time I read the story of The Fall I want to tell them not to do it, don't eat of that tree! But my cries fall on deaf pages.

It seems that Satan has won, Adam and Eve fall and God kicks them out of the Garden of Eden, tells them they will toil the Earth, childbirth will be painful and life will no longer be as it once was. Satan would have loved for the story to end there, but our God is a loving God and it doesn't end there. God doesn't stop talking to Adam and Eve, He still loves His creation and He wants them to know it.

Satan, of course, doesn't want them to know that God loves them. Satan strikes at men and women differently. Satan strikes at men through feelings of inadequacy, through a lack of strength. Satan strikes at the relational hearts of women. He strikes at the very things God loves about us because if we believe that God loves anything about us, we will surely begin to believe that God loves everything about us. When that happens, Satan will not only have lost the battle, but the war for our hearts and souls as well. So Satan strikes at our beauty, he causes us to doubt that we are truly beautiful, inside and out. He mocks our desire for our husbands, whether we know who they are yet or not. He attacks us by leading us to believe that we are never enough. We are not pretty enough, we are not thin enough, not smart enough, not tall enough, not hard-working enough, not, not, not. We just can't be. So the vicious cycle of lies continues, unless we are smart enough to get out of the cycle, recognize the lies for what they are, and try to move past them and heal from the hurt that has been perpetuated since The Fall.

Unseen

The Father of Lies has to start somewhere. If you believed, truly believed with all of your being, with all of your heart, your strength, your mind, and your soul that the God of the Universe loved you and held you in the palm of His hand, then Satan would be utterly defeated. Satan would have no hold on our hearts if we believed that God loved us as passionately as He does. Satan's biggest defense, one of his greatest weapons against us, is doubt. If he can get you to start doubting that God loves you then he begins to work his way into your heart and soul. He doesn't come at our hearts in big, obvious ways because then we would see him coming and avoid him. Satan is not the giant sink-hole in the street waiting for you to drive into it, we would simply drive around it. Satan isn't even the giant sink-hole in the middle of the street with an asphalt-colored tarp draped over it, for even that would be too obvious. Satan is far more like a tiny nail in the street that you drive over that pokes a tiny little hole in your tire. You don't realize you drove over the nail, and chances are you don't hear the air slowly leaking out of your tire. In time, though, your tire goes flat and Satan has hindered your ability to go anywhere or do anything with any amount of ease.

So, how can we avoid the nails in the road if we don't see them? Do we have to check our tires every night and listen for the leaks before we can go into our houses? Not necessarily. We need to learn to see clearly, to prepare ourselves for the nails and recognize them for what they are. We recognize them by starting with the first lies Satan tells us as women. Just as we learned as little kids, once you tell a lie you usually have to tell another lie to cover up the first one, and another lie to cover up the second lie, and on and on we go. So does Satan. We must uncover the lies and be aware that he uses them to build even more lies because his main and only goal is to keep us away from God, locked in a pit of desolation, just as he is.

The Initial Ache

Have you ever felt unnoticed? Unseen? Have you ever felt that no matter what you did no one would even take notice? You could put on the most beautiful dress, get your hair and make-up done, and still no heads would turn. You could dress like Julia Roberts in the opening scenes of *Pretty Woman* and there would be no Richard Gere there to pick you up in some fancy foreign car. We feel unseen. As women we long to be found beautiful, stunning, attractive, sexy. One of my favorite books sums up what we long for in the title: *Captivating.* We want to walk in a room and light it up. We want heads to turn, people to take notice that we are there and we are radiant. We possess within our very souls something magical, something mystical that shines and begs to be noticed. That isn't to say that every woman wants to be the center of attention when she walks in a room, many women do not. Some of my best friends would actually hate walking into a room and having everyone stare at her beauty. They would fear all the attention and wonder if they had something stuck in their teeth or that there is toilet paper stuck to their shoes. Those same women who don't want to be the center of attention will admit that they at least want one person to take note when they enter a room.

Satan knows this about the heart of women. What is the first lie that he often tells us? We are unseen. He whispers it to us,

"No one notices you. No one sees you. No one cares. There is fundamentally nothing at all that is special about you, and therefore no one bothers to take notice of you." We hear him and we begin to believe him.

How do we respond? We buy a nice perfume. We pick a lotion that makes our skin smell good and look shiny and smooth all day. We go to a tanning salon so we can look like we've just come back from the beach, even if it is the dead of winter. We dab on a little extra make-up. We spend a few extra minutes primping, curling our hair, shaving our legs, plucking our eyebrows, waxing our upper-lip, and picking out the perfect outfit. We throw on a pair of heels so we can be taller, and you know that heels make us look good when we finally figure out how to walk in them. God knows we all spent time in our younger years trying on our mother's, aunt's, and older sister's heels and tripping all over the place. We shower. We wear deodorant (I'm not saying that any of these things are bad or that Satan wins when we shower. Please, shower. I'm begging you. Wear deodorant, too.)

We think that if we put in the extra effort someone has to notice. Sometimes, they do, sometimes they don't. Sometimes, however, does not equal *every* time and this lack of consistent results is exactly where Satan hones in. When our efforts don't produce immediate results, or when we think they don't, Satan begins to creep in.

What comes next? We go shopping. We buy a new shirt, perhaps it is a little lower cut than everything else in our closet. Maybe it isn't quite as long as it should be and our stomachs peek out. We buy a new pair of jeans, the tight ones. We buy a higher pair of heels because maybe we weren't tall enough to be noticed before. We buy a skirt or a dress that shows off those nice legs that we spent so much time shaving, waxing, and tanning. Show off what God gave you, right? We walk in a room and this time we are looking for that shock factor, for someone's head to nearly snap off as they take in all that we are. Somehow, despite these changes, we still go unnoticed and our own disappointment grows, as does Satan's joy at his success at weaseling his way into our minds.

Where can we go from here? We start walking into different rooms. The situations we put ourselves in are different. The scenes we seek out are different. Maybe, we think, those people I spent time with before were just tired of seeing me. Maybe I need a new crowd, one that is more focused on looks and less on the "other stuff." Our shirts get lower, our jeans get tighter, our make-up gets more elaborate, our hair takes far longer to do and we smell like a goddess. We slowly make the transition from waiting to be noticed for our beauty to wanting to be "hot." We started out longing for beauty, for perfection. We want perfection because we were made for perfection; we were made in the image of Perfection. We long for Eden, our lost reality. In our attempts to be noticed we begin to give into the Fall, we sell ourselves out and instead we aim for the shock factor because we see that more instantaneously. Looking for the shock factor is a more tangible way to gauge our influence than being appreciated for our beauty and innocence.

To Be Used or to Be Appreciated

Pretty and beautiful have died and "hot" has replaced them. "Hot" in today's world is understood to be the shock factor, the "wow" we can't help but utter when we look at someone attractive. "Hot" is more focused on the physical appeal of a person which includes everything from their body to their clothes and hairstyle. Pat Archbold writes about this change in a blog called "The Death of Pretty" noting that most women no longer desire to be pretty. He writes, "Young women today do not seem to aspire to [be] pretty, they prefer to be regarded as hot. Hotness is something altogether different. When women want to be hot instead of pretty, they must view themselves in a certain way and consequently men view them differently as well."[1]

Archbold hit the nail on the head. We were made to know, understand and believe that we are *inherently* beautiful. We were made for the bare naked beauty we enjoyed in the Garden of Eden. When we aspire to hotness, our understanding of true beauty changes and is lessened. Anything outside of inherent beauty, beauty which needs no primping, no designer label, is less. Hotness is worthless when compared to beauty. Beauty is transcendent; it exists outside of time and place, it can, and often is, revered, adored, and worshipped regardless of culture, time, or place. The same can simply not be said of hotness. Hotness is relative, bound to time, culture, and place. The difference between beauty and hotness could be described as the difference between seeing the Mona Lisa in person and seeing it through a textured

---

[1] Archbold, Pat. "The Death of Pretty." *National Catholic Register*. EWTN News, 21 Dec. 2011. Web. <http://www.ncregister.com/blog/the-death-of-pretty>.

glass door. You may see the Mona Lisa through the glass but the image would be distorted and you wouldn't grasp the Mona Lisa's true beauty. Satan has wormed his way in and we have begun to believe that we must be hot if we are ever going to be noticed. "Forget about pretty, forget about beautiful," Satan says, "they don't get you noticed, they don't turn heads. Be hot, hot will get you noticed. Hot will turn heads." But is seeing the Mona Lisa through glass as beautiful and inspiring as seeing it with nothing blocking your view?

There is a problem with hot, many problems, in fact. When we think of heat we know and understand that it must be used, it must be consumed. Heat fades. A fire doesn't burn forever, unless we add more fuel to it. We try to add fuel to our hotness with plastic surgery, piles and piles of makeup, Botox, and the like. Heat's value is temporary, it is passing. Even the hottest flame can burn out quicker than we ever imagined; just add a bucket of water and the bonfire disappears. When we aspire to be hot instead of pretty, in essence we aspire to be used. Hotness is a fading thing, it is as temporary as the flame of a candle, when the wax runs out, the flame dies and we are left in the cold. When our hotness fades, when our youth escapes us, our use dies and we too are left in the cold.

Beauty is eternal and unchanging. No one doubts that the Mona Lisa or the Sistine Chapel are beautiful and wonderful to behold. People travel from all over the world to see such beautiful and timeless works of art. The sex symbols of our age are deemed hot and are constantly criticized. Think of the countless stars that we have deemed hot (or some variant of hot) over the years: Jessica Simpson, Elizabeth Taylor, Kelly Clarkson, Taylor Swift, Kristen Stewart, Katherine Hepburn, Julia Roberts, the list goes on. I can guarantee you that at some point over the course of their careers they have been criticized and judged for putting on weight, not wearing enough make-up, not showing enough skin, and more. Pick up any tabloid magazine if you don't believe me, reading only the cover will prove my point. Their hot factor is questioned because just as flames fade, their hotness fades, and ours will too.

Archbold continues, "Pretty is cherished. Hotness, on the other hand, is a commodity. Its value is temporary and must be used."[2] I'll say it again, hotness must be *used* and it is *temporary*. Do we, as women, aspire to be used and temporary? Not at all! It is a point that bears repeating: we were created for perfection, for eternity. Perfection never involved being used or taken advantage of. Eternity is not temporary or fleeting, quite the opposite by its very definition. We long to be cherished, to be valued and appreciated. The only reason we aspire to hotness is because it is the lie that Satan has sold us and we believe, hook, line and sinker. Hotness is the bait Satan so often uses to hook women and drag them down into his pit of never ending lies. Ask any woman (or man for that matter) for the God's honest truth and they would tell you that they don't really, in their heart of hearts, want to be used or temporary. No one wakes up in the morning and thinks to themselves, "I wonder how I can be used today. I hope more people use me today than yesterday." Such a thought is simply absurd. We long to be remembered, and to be eternal. We long to

---

[2] Ibid.

be cherished, to be held up and adored; we want to leave a glorious legacy on this earth. We want to be noticed, and yes, we want to turn heads, but deep down we want to turn heads because we offer the world something more intoxicating than fleeting, temporary hotness. We want our beauty to speak of and point to the eternal, to the God who created us, to Him whose beauty we reflect, whose beauty we were made in the image of. The notion of being used and temporary is sickening and it is a lie that must be exposed. Hotness may win the day today but eventually we will see the decline of hotness, and in its place will remain a cold, bitter shell of a once great beauty.

Archbold conjures up the image of Sandy, played by Olivia Newton John, in the classic movie and musical *Grease*. She starts out at the beginning of the movie full of beauty, innocence, and wonder. She is pretty. She is sweet, honest, and caring. By the end of the movie we see a transformation in her. In order to attract the attention of Danny Zuko, played by John Travolta, she changes. She becomes hot. She is clad in tight pants, shiny black leather clothing and hair big enough to make us wonder if she can fit through doorways. Because hotness is a consumable, it also consumes, in much the same way that a wildfire can ravage a forest. It consumes what was once a beautiful, young, innocent girl into a hot object that appears ready and willing for any number of activities the original Sandy would have never agreed to. I do mean *object*. She becomes less of a person to be upheld and appreciated and more of an object to be used and thrown out with yesterday's newspaper.

As a side note, it is important to note the change in Danny Zuko in *Grease*. He starts out the movie a rebel, a hooligan by most people's standards. He sees the beauty, the innocence of Sandy as she originally was and is challenged, and inspired by her, and changes for the better. He trades his hotness in for letterman's jackets and a clean-cut look that speaks more about who he is than the kind of trouble he is looking for. Beauty and innocence inspire, they can and do challenge others (men and women) to be better versions of themselves. Hotness challenges no one; it brings out the parts of us that seek to use others and to be used.

A study of male college students at Princeton University revealed that when males looked at photographs of scantily clad women, the part of their brain that is associated with tool use lit up the most. Rather than viewing these women as people, the male brain associated these immodestly dressed women with first person verbs such as "I push, handle, grab, etc."[3] Women, when immodestly dressed, are more commonly seen as objects rather than people. Consequently, men are not challenged, much less invited, to appreciate and defend our feminine beauty. When we aspire to hotness we are not only being used, we are using others. We look to them for validation and for gratification. We use their stares, their attention to feel good about ourselves. Use only perpetuates more use.

---

[3] Evert, Jason. "Is It Wrong to Wear a Bikini?" *Chastity.com*. Catholic Answers. <http://www.chastity.com/chastity-qa/how-far-too-far/modesty/it-wrong-wear-bikini/it->.

The Flame that Consumes

Hotness lowers our standards and the way we see ourselves as women, and in turn changes the way that men see us. It also changes us into a commodity that begs to be used, but worse still, it consumes us. Archbold states, "Hotness is a consumable. A consumable that consumes as it is consumed but brings no warmth."[4] Just as Sandy's innocence was consumed in *Grease*, so too our innocence is consumed when we trade beauty for hotness; it consumes us as we are consumed by it. The warmth that Archbold is referring to is the warmth that comes from a happy, peaceful, joy-filled soul, not one that is aching and constantly seeking attention and validation from others. When we are warm, we are loving and giving, not selfish and needy. As the cycle of use continues any and all perceived warmth from our hotness dies. Blessed Pope John Paul II taught that the opposite of hatred is not love, it is use. Love is warm, a true and undying flame, while use is cold. A fire doesn't burn forever unless we add fuel to it. With hotness there is no true, lasting fuel that can be added to it to keep our flame burning. Time will have its way with us and the clothes that were once skin tight will barely hold us in, our make-up will go out of style, and our hotness will be gone forever.

Hotness is a slippery slope. It starts with a little extra make-up, some extra time doing our hair and then it degenerates into tighter, more revealing clothes and, usually, all of the activities that go with those tight, revealing clothes. Take this hotness

---

[4] Archbold, Pat. "The Death of Pretty." *National Catholic Register*. EWTN News, 21 Dec. 2011. Web. <http://www.ncregister.com/blog/the-death-of-pretty>.

business to its extreme and it is exactly the same as a burning candle. In time, our need to be hot will consume us and we will forget our original glory, our original created dignity. We will be left with a closet full of clothes that barely fit us – on one end of the spectrum or another – and, tons and tons of make-up and yet we will still be unhappy, we will still not be warm. We will still be unseen. Then, as our hotness fades because it too is being consumed, we will fade with it. We doubt that we will ever be seen, we doubt that we will ever be noticed or appreciated. We begin to long for the way things were, the days when we had our innocence, when at least we found ourselves pretty. We long for those days and yet Satan whispers to us that those days are gone, they are over, we sold them, we traded our innocence for them and we can't ever get them back, no matter how hard we try.

The Nail in the Coffin

Satan has almost got us; he has nearly won this lie. He only needs to drive that final nail home. He has to get this lie into the depths of our hearts. He has led us to trade our beauty, our innocence, for hotness. We have begun to sell ourselves short and we allow others to sell us short as well.

Look at TV shows over the past few decades. There was a time when even married couples, like Lucy and Ricky on *I Love Lucy*, who were actually married in real life, weren't allowed to be shown sleeping in the same bed in their own home. Such a picture was too scandalous to show on television. Yet, here we are some 55 years after the end of *I Love Lucy* and we have television shows that not only show married couples in bed together, they feature such scenes regularly. Then there are shows that feature cheating outside of marriage for nothing more than entertainment's sake. There are shows, many, many shows in which the characters regard adultery and fornication as normal. We tune in week after week to watch a bachelor or bachelorette date multiple people at once on what is frequently referred to as a "game show," as if love were something to be won. If we tune in often enough we begin to believe that adultery, fornication, porn within marriage, or porn at all, are good and morally acceptable.

How does Satan drive his nail in our coffin of hotness, in our coffin of being unseen? He sets the project in motion and he watches, laughs maniacally (or at least I imagine that he does) as we are consumed by our hotness, and as it consumes us. His nail in our coffins is to get us to believe that it is too late to change our ways. Inevitably we will reach a point where we want things to be the way they were, to be appreciated and honored, not used and consumed. Perhaps things were never really great, but they must have been better than being used and consumed. We at least want to believe that if we changed, then things would get better, we would feel less used and more appreciated. At some point such a desire will enter our hearts. Satan drives his nail in the coffin by getting us to stifle that thought, to shove that desire away. He gets us to believe that even if we changed ourselves, our hearts, our attitude, and our wardrobe no one would care. The damage, he leads us to believe, has been done. It is too late for us, we waited too long to want more for ourselves. We are on the road of no return and there are no U-turns to be found. Satan leads us to believe that once the world sees us as hot it will never again see us as beautiful, nor will anyone ever appreciate us for who we are, instead of what we can do with our bodies and our sex appeal. We are led to believe that we have gone too far down this road of hotness; the wax of hope, innocence, and beauty that once filled our hearts, allowing them to burn brightly, is depleted and cannot be restored. We gave up our innocence, we gave up our beauty, we gave up our naïveté, and those are things we believe – or at least Satan wants us to believe – that we can never get back. Ever. Satan takes the nail and drives it into our coffins, and we submit to lay in the dark coffin, hopeless, utterly defeated, and unseen.

Unsought

We have already been locked away in our coffins of hotness, in the coffin of being unseen, how much worse could it get? Much worse. I used to think that if we simply didn't ask the "How much worse can it get?" question then it couldn't and wouldn't get worse. Oh, how I wish that were true. If only Satan were content at locking us in one coffin and leaving us there the story would be over and we would wither away in that coffin forever. But Satan is not content with one coffin. He needs more safeguards than that. Satan is paranoid and his paranoia serves him well. He needs to be sure we will never escape his grip. He needs us to feel as though he has won, to feel as though he has taken something away from God. The thought of losing us, of not locking us up tightly enough, is a thought that is too painful for Satan to bear. He seeks to lock us away in a series of coffins, a bit like a set of Russian dolls. The coffin of being unseen is only the first in a series of coffins that Satan is determined to keep placing around our hearts until he is sure that we will never escape his confinement. Truth, Satan expects, will never make its way into our hearts releasing us from bondage. Satan hates our beautiful, feminine hearts just as much as God loves them. Satan will never be content with simply winning our hearts over, he must bury them, lock them away until they are dead, with nope hope for resurrection. Our hearts must never be awakened by true love's kiss, they must never be roused by some magic potion, nor any amount of life or goodness. They must remain locked away and buried until the darkness sucks every last ounce of life from them.

The Search

Stasi Eldredge states it quite well in *Captivating*: "We feel *unsought* – that no one has the passion or the courage to pursue us, to get past our messiness to find the woman deep inside us."[1] Doesn't that statement make our hearts wake up and say, scream, and shout with joy, "YES!" We already feel as if no one notices us as women; no one upholds us or appreciates our beauty. We are locked in a coffin of being unseen and the next coffin has a nice, shiny label: Unsought. The difference is a subtle one, but there is a difference nonetheless. To be unseen is to simply go unnoticed. To be unsought, on the other hand, is to have no one searching for our feminine hearts. To be unseen is passive, no one took the time to look up and notice us, and it takes little to no actual effort to notice us. To be unsought is far more active, because it requires a search, a quest, a hunt, an adventure to find us. We feel that no one has the passion, the courage, the will, the drive, or the motivation to truly seek us out, to search for our hearts. We have lost our ability to believe that we are inherently beautiful because we've been locked in a coffin of hotness. We believe that no matter what we do we will always be unseen. The mess has already begun and because we've bought into, even crawled into that first coffin, we have given Satan a foothold. It is only a matter of time until he continues to build more coffins around us. We believe that we are messy and unseen, so, if no one bothers to notice us, why on earth would someone, anyone, actually search for us, for our hearts?

---

[1] Eldredge, John & Stasi. *Captivating*. Nashville, TN: Thomas Nelson, 2005. 7.

Branches that Bind

When I think about the coffins that Satan continually locks us in, I think of the Whomping Willow tree in the *Harry Potter* series. The tree has many arms which move and capture those who come close to it. The branches reach out and grab onto your foot and whip you around for a bit before latching on to your arms, your torso, whatever it possibly can. Satan works in much the same way. He grabs our feet and immobilizes us. He grabs our hands, covers our mouths and slowly takes us over until we completely give up hope. It sounds depressing because it is, which is exactly what Satan wants.

It is here, in the coffin of Unsought, that we begin to lock up our own hearts. We may have let Satan lead us into the coffin of Unseen, but once we were nailed and locked inside that first coffin we began, however slowly, to give up hope. Maybe the breakdown of our hope was gradual, maybe it was intentional, and maybe it happened fast and followed the final nail being hammered into the coffin of Unseen. Either way, we began to follow Satan more readily – whether we realized it or not – and we began to follow him down this road that only leads to more coffins. We begin to build walls around our own hearts because we foolishly think that if we can build the walls high enough, strong enough, and thick enough, we won't feel the pain of being unseen and unsought. Satan sees that we are building these walls around our hearts and he devilishly laughs, and, like the Whomping Willow, he grabs ahold of another one of our limbs. Locked away behind these walls, our hearts will be safe, or so we are led to believe. Alexander Pope once wrote, "Blessed is the man who expects nothing, for he shall never be disappointed."[2] At first glance that sounds like a wonderful idea, who doesn't want to be blessed? Pope wrote that may as well have been the ninth, or perhaps the "forgotten" beatitude in Jesus' Sermon on the Mount.[3] It was forgotten for a reason: it too easily leaves out hope. There is a fine line between hope and expectations. When we hope, we wait with excited anticipation. When we expect, the line becomes blurred and the expectations become more engrained in who we are. Expectations lead us to wait in anticipation, but we wait believing that we *deserve* whatever it is we are waiting for. Pride blurs the lines between hope and expectation. To hope is a wonderful, beautiful thing. It is one of the theological virtues Saint Paul speaks about so often in his letters. To expect is to look for something with reason or justification; we hold this line of expectation because we feel we deserve something on our own merits.

We don't want to be disappointed. How can we possibly get to a point where we don't expect anything from anyone, ever? We must kill our hearts. We must kill our souls. Our hearts desire happiness, our souls desire peace and joy. In order to arrive at a place where we expect nothing, we must stifle and bury our hearts because we believe our hearts lead us to expect goodness. Satan may as well wrap another proverbial branch around us and drive another nail into yet another coffin.

---

[2] Williams, Howard, Jonathan Swift, and Alexander Pope. *English Letters and Letterwriters of the Eighteenth Century. With Explanatory Notes.* London: G. Bell & Sons, 1886. 466.

[3] Ibid.

This lack of expectations could very well be its own coffin. We lock our hearts away because we don't want to be continually disappointed in the world and the people around us. Disappointment, if it came on its own, would be something we could probably handle. But disappointment, like misery, loves company. Disappointment brings with it anger, resentment, bitterness, hatred, frustration, sadness, and depression. Disappointment is like a branch on the Whomping Willow that has ten more branches coming off of the original branch. It is a life-sucker. It takes away our hope that anything could ever turn out well. We build up the walls around our hearts to keep out the disappointment and as we do so we also begin the long road of surrendering to despair, to darkness and to hopelessness. The disappointment we've felt at being unseen and unsought breeds in our hearts and it grows, it becomes like a tumor and we believe that the only way to get rid of the tumor is to take out our whole heart. We fear that if we leave any part of our heart behind that the tumor will continue to grow. We throw the baby out with the bath water.

False Hope

What happens if someone, by some miracle of the universe, some unexpected grace, some unforeseen lightning bolt of hope, does happen to actually notice us? We might begin to hope, to believe that things could improve in our lives. We might think that because someone noticed us, they might actually search for us. The logic side of our brains spring to life and jump to exciting and hope-filled conclusions. This person might be our knight in shining armor riding in on a beautiful white horse to save us from our fate, to break open the walls we've built around our hearts and tear down the coffin that Satan has nailed us into. We might begin to believe that this person is the long awaited hope who has the passion and the drive to seek us out, to wade their way through the messiness of our lives and actually appreciate who we are. We might begin to believe.

Now we see why Satan needs multiple coffins to lock us in. Someone notices, some head finally, after this long struggle, turns and takes notice of us. It would seem, at least at first glance, a glimmer of hope finally shines upon us. However, we are already locked in the coffin of Unseen and well on our way to letting Satan drive the final nail into the coffin of Unsought. That look, that glance, that simple head turn isn't enough. Pride, the very fault that Satan used to get Eve to eat the forbidden fruit, has come in and taken hold of our hearts and we don't *just* want to be noticed, we want someone to search for us. Having *nearly* everything in the Garden of Eden wasn't enough for Eve, and so having *nearly* enough is not good enough for us either. Eve wanted more than a life of eternal ease and bliss with Adam and God, she wanted to eat of the tree that had been forbidden. She thought God was holding out on her. We, the daughters of Eve, want more than a little glance. A glance may have been enough to fill our hearts with hope a few months or years ago, but it is too late and this coffin has gotten too dark to be filled by the tiny light of some happenstance, potentially chance glance in our direction. The more we believe it is too late for that glance to be enough for us, the more readily we let Satan drive the final nails into the coffin of Unsought.

The Poison in the Vice

Pride, just as it taught Eve to want more, teaches us to want more. What is more alarming, however, is that pride not only teaches us to want more, it teaches us to believe that we deserve more. G.K. Chesterton believed that pride is the poison in every other vice. Pride is the king of the vices and it infects and motivates every other vice. Chesterton also said, "There are two ways to get enough. One is to continue to accumulate more and more. The other is to desire less."[4] We can easily see for ourselves which road pride leads us down: the same one we have been on since Adam and Eve were kicked out of the Garden of Eden. We want more and more. What we fail to realize, at least not yet anyway, is that no matter how much we acquire it will never be enough. Unfortunately, it is usually a long, dark, winding road that we travel down before we realize that the real option that will make us happy is the second option offered to us by Chesterton: to desire less. Instead, we keep crawling, walking, and running down this road of more. We don't want just a glance now. We don't want to just be noticed. We don't want to just be appreciated for our beauty alone, for the way we dress or the way we look. We want someone to search for us, to seek us, to intentionally and passionately hunger for us.

No Reason to Believe

The first coffin, we believe, is sealed. If no one ever notices us, even in only a vain or purely physical way, we have no reason to believe that anyone would ever actively search for us.

---

[4] As quoted in Farrar, Steve, and Mary Farrar. *Overcoming Overload*. Sisters, OR: Multnomah, 2003. 168.

Just as Satan's lies build on one another, so does our hope. We know that in order for someone to search for us, they must first see us. If someone, even just one person, saw us, took note of our beauty early on, then we would have reason to believe that maybe, just maybe, someday, somewhere someone (hopefully on a white horse, of course) would actually seek us out and search for our hearts. If someone took notice, then perhaps that someone would have the courage, the passion, and the motivation to intentionally search for us, to wade their way through the mess of our lives and find the woman buried deep within.

Just as Satan needs a foundation on which to build his lies and seal us in our coffins, we need a foundation upon which to build our hope that things can get better. If we fail to be noticed in even the smallest and most shallow way, then we have no concrete foundation to hope that anyone will ever search for us, much less pursue us or love us for who we are. We listen to songs like the popular Jesse McCartney song "Beautiful Soul" and laugh, because who would want a beautiful soul if they don't first take a second to notice a beautiful woman? It sounds nice. Oh, sure, it sounds wonderful. But when we get to the point where we feel we aren't noticed at all, we hear those lyrics and by time they make their way to our brains they sound more like, "I don't see your pretty face because you don't have one, I don't want to hold you because I refuse to notice you, my love would be wasted on you, I want a beautiful soul and yours is quite ugly." We, as women, have no reason to believe such sweet lyrics could ever be sung about us because time and time again no one bothers to notice us. We simply go unnoticed, and we begin to believe that we always will be unnoticed. As our disappointment at being constantly unnoticed and unsought grows, so do the walls around our hearts.

If, by some miracle, someone does notice us, we may begin to hope, but it won't be enough for us. Instead, we begin to play games like hard-to-get. We become elusive; we test their glances and their flirtatious stares. We see that certain someone noticing us, so we disappear and reappear in the room or in their lives because we are testing how deeply and intentionally they notice us. We disappear and reappear because we are hoping that eventually they will search for us. We hope that they won't allow us to disappear anymore. We hope that they will see us and will hunger for us, that they will want more of us. So as we play this game of cat-and-mouse our hopes come back to life because we hope that this person who has noticed us will then search for us, make of us an adventure, a prize to search for and follow after. Satan allows a tiny bit of hope into our first coffin because, in time, we will inevitably be disappointed.

We play cat-and-mouse, we play hard-to-get, we play countless other games to test the glances and affections of that person who happened to see us, but we are left disappointed when they don't search for us. They don't come after us. They may chat with us for a time but they never ask for our phone numbers so that they can continue the conversation. We find out they are married, they were drunk and looking for a cheap hook up (our pride has gotten too big to allow for such cheap tricks), or, perhaps worse, that they were actually looking at some girl standing next to us, and we foolishly let ourselves believe that we were the object of their affectionate glances. They don't search for us, they simply let us disappear once again. The games are over and that little light, that tiny glimmer of hope that once entered our coffins, has gone too and we are left in darkness, a darkness that is deeper and more profound than before. Here, in the desolate darkness we submit to the first coffin. We welcome its now familiar darkness, and the cold comfort we find within its walls. We begin to see at this point that the only thing or person that notices us is Satan (or at least we are led to believe this is true; remember, Satan is the Father of Lies). We see that Satan is the only one searching for us, so we return to him, and we submit to him. We begin to trust him because the only attention we seem to be getting is from him. We see that he knows we will be disappointed and we take this as a truth from him. We start to believe his words and promises and fail to see how empty they are. So we lock our hearts away, giving up hope that anyone else will ever notice us, giving up hope that anyone else will ever search for us, and we allow Satan to seal our second coffin: Unsought.

Unpursued

Much like Hell in Dante Alighieri's famous *Inferno* in the epic poem *Divine Comedy*, Satan's lies have layers to them. The same is said about ogres in the movie *Shrek*, as the title character explains that ogres are like onions, they have layers. Donkey tries to convince Shrek that other things have layers and are far more enjoyable than onions. Donkey suggests that ogres could be like parfaits: they have layers but are tasty, and everyone loves them. Shrek disagrees, ogres are not like parfaits, rather, ogres are like onions, plain and simple. Not everyone likes onions, nor does everyone like ogres. The same is true about Satan's lies. They could be like a parfait, a sweet and tasty treat, and his lies lure us in with their empty promises, but there is nothing sweet and tasty about Satan's lies. I, too, dislike onions. I've never really been fond of onions, which is why this metaphor works so well for me, my apologies if you enjoy onions. Satan's lies are far more like an onion, they don't smell good, I don't think they taste good, no matter how you cook or prepare them, and they certainly don't leave you with a good taste in your mouth. Their odor hangs around and clouds your breath long after they are gone and digested. Similarly, Satan's lies don't smell good, they don't taste good and they don't leave you with a good taste in your mouth. Also, they hang around and cloud your mind long after they are taken in.

In order to expose the lies, we must keep descending. The layers of Hell in Dante's *Inferno* only increase in severity and horrifying images as the reader descends into them. The same is true about our journey, the layers and the lies will not get any prettier the further we descend, but in order to expose them, in order to bring light into the darkness, we must keep descending, all the while increasing our own awareness of Satan's lies and tricks, lest the dark pit consume us whole. Plug your nose if you must, for the journey to the center of the metaphorical onion continues.

The Mission with a Goal

Satan has already led us to believe that we are unseen and unsought. Again we ask the question, how much worse could it get? Could there really be any more coffins that Satan wants to lock our hearts away in? When we start asking those questions, Satan starts laughing. If you are quiet enough you might even hear him snicker in his maniacal little way. Of course there are more coffins, of course there are more lies he can sell us. He isn't done with us until our hearts are dead and we believe that we can never be redeemed. Until we reach that day he'll keep selling us on more lies and more coffins.

What is worse than being unsought is being unpursued. Being unpursued goes deeper than being unsought. To be unseen is to have no one notice you. To be unsought is to have no one search after you. To be unpursued means all of the above, and that no one has a deeper mission. The definition of pursuing as a verb means to look for with a mission, with a purpose of winning over, or to woo with the intent to captivate or take over. To be pursued is a beautiful thing, it makes a woman come alive, which is exactly why Satan wants us to believe that we are unpursued, and we always will be. There is something enchanting about being pursued because the pursuit goes so much deeper than a simple glance or someone searching for you, it is more than a knight in shining armor coming to your house. To be pursued is to have a knight in shining armor come to your house with the sole purpose of winning your heart over, of wooing you, of captivating you, of finding you beautiful and making you his closest and most intimate companion for the rest of his days.

    Think of all of your favorite girly movies. Almost every girly movie has a main male character and at some point in the movie, even if it is only for a few scenes, he pursues the woman. Richard Gere rides in a white limo and calls out to Julia Roberts as she stands on a balcony in *Pretty Woman*. Gere runs after Julia Roberts after she hops aboard a FedEx truck when she runs away from their wedding in *Runaway Bride*. Noah builds Allie her dream house, hoping and praying that she will come home to it someday in *The Notebook*. Keanu Reeves defies the confines of time when at last he is in the same year and place with Sandra Bullock in *The Lake House*. Matthew McConaughey fights traffic to stop Kate Hudson from leaving town in *How To Lose A Guy In 10 Days*. Name a chick-flick and I can almost guarantee you there is a scene in it with a man riding in on a proverbial (or a real) white horse to woo the woman of his dreams. The same is true of the books we read. Ron finally, *finally* gives in and kisses Hermoine in the final installment of the *Harry Potter* books, and what an epic kiss we all imagined it to be. Landon Carter gives up his bad boy ways and takes Jamie Sullivan on a beautiful date in Nicholas Sparks' *A Walk to Remember*. The guys that don't pursue the women in movies and books we call pigs, jerks, boys (in the most derogatory voice we can muster), scum bags, and a whole host of other nasty terms. We want them to stand up, to notice us, to search for us and to pursue us with passion and purpose. When they fail to do so we rail against them, we call them names, we tear them down and we shoot them every mean glare and stink eye in the book.

In all of the great love stories the man pursues the woman, time after time, book after book, and movie after movie. Writers put it in movies and authors put it in books because the story line sells. Why? Because it speaks to our feminine hearts and we eat it up, every single time. My favorite romantic movie is *Pride & Prejudice*. Mr. Darcy pursues Lizzy with a passion and a purpose that is tireless and unmatched by any other character in any other movie I have ever seen. My college girlfriends and I would spend countless hours talking and dreaming about our own real-life Mr. Darcys. That kind of pursuit is something our feminine hearts long for and are willing to wait for. We want to be pursued, whether it is by friends who actually want to spend time with us, or by a man who wants to get to know us, to work past our messiness and find the woman deep within. We long for it, and Satan rails against it.

The Slippery Slope Gets Slicker

We keep buying the lies. In each chapter so far we've seen what happens when we buy into the lies. Our wardrobe changes and becomes more revealing. Our make-up goes on thicker. The crowd we hang out with changes. We keep wondering just how much worse it can get. How can this slippery slope get any slicker? Then it hits us; with our change of wardrobe and change of make-up and change of crowd, our values begin to change.

It usually starts small: our vocabulary changes. A once clean mouth slowly slips into a mouth that any self-respecting grandmother would love to wash out with a giant bar of the worst tasting soap she could find. Maybe we don't use the typical foul words that aren't allowed on public television. Maybe our mouth oozes out innuendos, lewd terms, and the like. We refer to things, body parts, and other people using the most demeaning and offensive words we can think of. We invent new words to describe and tear down other people. We use slang in the place of commonly understood words. We drag others down with us. Besides, if we are going to be locked in a coffin or two, or three or four, why not lock others in there with us? Misery loves company.

I had a teacher in high school that used to say that there was no place, rhyme or reason for foul language; it only showed a person's ignorance. He was and is absolutely right. If we, as humans with vast resources at our fingertips, can't find a way to express ourselves and describe the world around us using terms that don't intentionally seek to offend other people then we show our true colors, and we show our ignorance. There is always a way to express ourselves using words that don't undermine our message. When we continue to use language that is said for its shock value and with the intent of offending others, we usually find that we don't fit in with the crowd we once did, so we change crowds. We find people who talk like us and aren't offended by our potty mouths, nor do they care to wash them out with soap. The slippery slope gets more slippery; perhaps it is from all that unused soap that we should be washing our mouths out with.

We find people who are like us and because their mouths are like ours, we start to change our hearts to match theirs as well. When we find that our usual crowd no longer accepts what we believe to be a new and improved version of ourselves it is easy to grow very bitter toward them. Naturally when we find a new crowd that bitterness will come out. Our hearts continue to grow colder and become even less connected to warmth and feeling. Void of friends who have our best interests at heart, our own hearts continue to barrel down the path lined with coffins. Our mouths change, our hearts change, and so do our values. In order to fit in with our new crowd we make sure that we are like them, we don't want to be left out in the cold again. We already feel unseen and unsought and we feel that ache in the depths of our hearts. We can't bear to feel the ache again from yet another group of friends.

I've heard far too many sad tales about how these new crowds lead to more drinking, more partying and then to more sleeping around. I know the tales and I am willing to bet you know them too; perhaps you are even living in them right now. Perhaps you are watching your best friend, your sister or someone else you care deeply about spiral downward. The people you care about recount their stories for you the morning after, and they are proud of how drunk they were, they are proud of the fact that they blacked out sooner than they ever had before. Your friends are proud of how long their hangover lasted, or perhaps they are proud of the fact that they are still drunk or hungover. You hear stories about how proud they are of how many guys they gave their number to, texted, sexted, kissed, made out with, hooked up with, and slept with. Your friends brag about how awesome their weekend is. In some cases they will tell you not to tell so-and-so, whether it is their mother, their older brother, their supposed boyfriend or the goodie-two-shoes down the block. Even so, they will still brag and carry on about their weekend as if they are having the time of their life.

I should know. I do know. I've been there. I had a semester in college (and I thank God it didn't last any longer than that) where I lived a double life. On the outside I looked like the angel child, I went to daily Mass, I went to confession weekly, I played and sang in the choir at the student Mass, and I knew each of the monks by name. I called home nearly every day and kept in touch with friends that were thousands of miles away. My grades were the best they had ever been up to that point and I held down a part-time job in addition to a full-time class load. Once the sun went down my life was a different story. I felt that I was in the prime of my youth and yet no guy was noticing me, no guy was searching for me or seeking me out and there were certainly no guys pursuing me. I decided to take matters into my own hands. I figured out pretty quickly that if I dressed a certain way guys would buy me drinks. If I dressed a different kind of a certain way and flirted with the right guys, then they would buy me what I wanted to drink, not just the cheap disgusting stuff (as if I really cared what I drank as long as I drank). I spent my days as an angel and my nights unleashing the devil within. I knew which friends I could brag to about the parties I'd been at and the guys I hooked up with. I also knew which friends not to tell. My story isn't uncommon. Sadly, it is all too common. I spent countless nights out late partying, including nights that my relatives had flown halfway across the country to spend with me, hanging out with people who didn't really care about me; they cared far more about corrupting my good girl image. What's worse is that I let them.

We know there is a hole in our hearts and we try to fill it with just about anything we can get our hands on, no matter how tightly Satan seems to have nailed our coffins shut. I knew there was a hole in my heart, a gaping hole. I wanted to be seen, to be sought out, to be pursued. None of that happened on my time table so I turned the table upside down and sought attention, and I got it. No matter how much I tried to fill the hole in my heart with partying, drinking, or the temporary, superficial affection from guys, I still felt that hole, just as big as it ever was. That was the beginning of my own downfall. That was when I began to not only let Satan nail me in my own coffin, I gave him the hammer and the nails and told him to have at it. I didn't want to feel pain or feel the hole in my heart anymore. I was done.

My values changed with my new crowd of 'friends'. God knows they were never really my friends, nor did they have my best interests at heart. They were interested in using me and I was interested in the attention they gave me, no matter how fleeting, shallow, or superficial that attention was. The fact that my values changed to match my new crowd only made it easier for Satan to nail more coffins around my heart. He began to show me how big that hole was and it felt so big that all I wanted to do was be closed off to it, so I handed him the hammer and the nails, laid down in my coffin and listened as he nailed me in, thankful to finally be closed off and taken away from that gaping hole in my heart.

Outside of Heaven

I wanted love but I didn't know how to find it. I wanted love but I didn't want the risk of putting my heart on the line, of opening up to someone and being truly vulnerable. To me, love simply wasn't worth the risk. I wanted a guarantee that if I put my heart out there that it would be safe, and that it would never be broken. I wanted to know, beyond the shadow of a doubt that my vulnerability, my willingness to fall in love would be rewarded. I wanted all of the reward and none of the risk. It wasn't until years later that I stumbled upon the book *The Four Loves* by C.S. Lewis. Had I found it in my drinking and partying days I think I would have laughed at what he wrote. I would have thought I was above it. I would have thought that surely I could have found a way to love without risking anything. Lewis brilliantly writes about love and the risks involved noting,

> "There is no safe investment. To love at all is to be vulnerable. Love anything, and your heart will be wrung and possibly broken. If you want to make sure of keeping it intact, you must give your heart to no one, not even to an animal. Wrap it carefully round with hobbies and little luxuries; avoid all entanglements; lock it up safe in the casket or coffin of your selfishness. But in that casket – safe, dark, motionless, airless – it will change. It will not be broken; it will become unbreakable, impenetrable, irredeemable. The alternative to tragedy, is damnation. The only place outside Heaven where you can be perfectly safe from all the dangers and perturbations of love is Hell."[1]

---

[1] Lewis, C. S. "Charity." *The Four Loves*. Orlando, FL: Harcourt, 1960. 121.

Over the years I heard bits and pieces of this quote, but until I read all of it I don't think I fully understood Lewis' immeasurable wisdom. The first two sentences alone are enough to make me recoil, yet they are brimming with truth. There is no safe investment. Satan repeatedly attempts to offer us one safe investment after another. We begin to believe that a coffin is a safe investment. Inside it we cannot be hurt, the pain will eventually subside and we will be free. Surely we want freedom, so this investment in coffins, in being nailed inside casket after casket after casket is a safe investment. Surely.

Lewis continues and reminds us of the most fundamental truth about love: it requires vulnerability. A person can be vulnerable and not love, but a person cannot love without being vulnerable, otherwise the love is not true. If we love anything, even an animal, Lewis quips, our hearts will be wrung and possibly broken. Love even your favorite sports team and they are bound to miss the crucial free throw, the game winning touchdown, or the easy goal on the open net. Love your favorite athlete and they'll commit a felony, they will break a bone, twist an ankle, or they'll retire someday. Love your dog and one day it will die. Love your computer and it will crash. Love a restaurant and the health department will find rats in the kitchen. Love anything and your heart will be wrung and possibly shattered.

If you want your heart to be safe then you must not give it away to anything or anyone. Not even the plant on your desk. Wrap your heart up, Lewis says, wrap it up in the nice little things of life. Wrap it in a nice job, though you mustn't get too attached to that corner office. Wrap it in a nice car, though you should have a good insurance policy. Wrap it in nice, brand name clothes. Wrap it in waking up early to enjoy a cup of coffee. Wrap it in the nice things in life, because perhaps once it is wrapped it will be safe – or so you will think. After all, even Lewis recognized that in order to be safe, in order to keep our hearts intact, we must lock them in coffins and caskets. We lock our hearts away in our own selfishness. Don't think it is selfishness? You've just been duped by Pride. Pride says you deserve to be seen, you deserve to be sought after, and you deserve to be pursued. Pride and selfishness all too often go hand in hand. Pride tells you what you think you deserve, and then you selfishly pursue that which you believe you are entitled to. We are locked in the coffin of our own selfishness. We have reached a point where we not only allow Satan to lock us away here, but we readily hand over the tools and tell him to be done with the project already, we are tired of playing his games.

Lewis also recognized that even when our hearts are locked away they can, and still do, change. We think that our hearts are safe in that "dark, motionless, airless" coffin as Lewis describes it. We think our hearts are done changing. They may be done hurting (or so Satan leads us to believe) but they are not done changing. Inside that coffin our hearts become "unbreakable, impenetrable, irredeemable." Our hearts become a steel cage, cold, unwelcoming, uninviting and all together uninspiring. Our hearts no longer point to the God who created us, now they point to the one who enslaves us.

The worst part of the changes in our hearts is that we believe we are irredeemable. We are sold yet another lie from the

Father of Lies and we buy into it. Satan wants nothing more for us than for us to buy into the lie that we can never, ever, *ever* be redeemed. If we believe that no one and nothing could ever redeem us, then it follows that we believe that no one could ever see us, search for us, pursue us, much less love us. If we are irredeemable then we also believe we are too ugly, too far gone for a fairy tale ending to this life, or to the next life. God never wanted to damn us, and, for that fact, He never wanted to damn Satan to hell for all of eternity. Scripture is a love letter from God, it is His lament for His people, His cry for us to return to Him.[2] He longs for our welfare, not for our woe.[3] We are, however, sold yet another lie from Satan: that we can never be redeemed. If we cannot be redeemed, then Jesus had no point in coming. Jesus becomes a laughing stock. Then, not only has Satan won our hearts, but he has even more reason to laugh at, scorn, mock, and belittle the Son of God.

Satan mocking the Son of God is nothing new, but it leads perfectly into Lewis' next thought, "The alternative to tragedy, is damnation." We buy into this lie, too. We choose –consciously or unconsciously – damnation over the tragedy of continued heartbreak, and the continuing ache of that never-satisfied hole in our hearts. We believe we are, by this point, too far gone for anything but damnation. We are far outside of Heaven and we have no real hope, no hope of returning or being invited to Heaven. With Heaven so far away we latch on to the next easiest

---

[2] Joel 2:12, Jer. 4:1, Neh. 1:9.

[3] Jer. 29:11.

solution to fix or stop our aching hearts: we lock them away in Hell.

C.S. Lewis had it exactly right, our hearts can only be safe in one of two places: Heaven or Hell. There is no in-between place where it can be safe. We can't put our hearts in a bunker somewhere, we can't bury them away in the sands of Egypt, and we can't place them in a lock-box for safe keeping. We believe we have lost Heaven. After all, if we were anywhere close to Heaven wouldn't someone notice us by now? Wouldn't someone search for us? Wouldn't someone pursue us? Because we are left unseen, unsought, and unpursued we conclude that we are nowhere near Heaven. The closest option for the protection and safe-keeping of our hearts is Hell (as if the misconstrued logic isn't evident in that statement alone). Fyodor Dostoevsky said, "God and the devil are fighting…and the battlefield is the heart of man."[4] The stage is set, the actors have arrived and are in full costume. No one yet knows if this play will be a tragedy, a comedy, or a mixture of both. Our hearts can only be safe in one of two places and the choice is ours. The classic scene of the devil on one shoulder and the angel on the other is before us. They are fighting and we all too easily side with the devil, we buy into his lies and we get sucked down into his bottomless pit. Damnation precludes hope, which is exactly what Satan wants. Satan hoped to reign supreme with God, to be equal with God. Because Satan's hopes were smashed, ours must be too in order for him to succeed in his devilish mission. The coffin he is locking us in must be dark. Actually, dark wouldn't be good enough. The darkness must

---

[4] Dostoevsky, Fyodor. *The Brothers Karamozov*. New York: Macmillan, 1922. 110.

increase. It must be darker than the darkest night we could ever imagine. The darkness must be void of light, hope, and love. Light must never penetrate; hope must never shine on us again.

To believe that we will never be pursued by anything or anyone is to nearly be dead. Satan's mission is almost over; our hearts are almost dead as they lay cold, alone, and motionless in coffin after coffin. We have allowed ourselves to be closed off, and we have closed our hearts off from light, hope and love. We try to shield ourselves from pain, anguish, and the unending aching in our hearts, but in so doing we have also closed our hearts off from the good things in life: joy, happiness, and peace. So it is that we remain locked in the Hell we believe we have created for ourselves, the Hell that we believe we have doomed and damned ourselves to for eternity.

Unworthy

Have you begun to feel it? Are you reading these chapters, continually wondering how many more lies Satan could possibly sell you, only to turn the page to read about more lies? We must expose them all if we ever hope to be truly free of the lies. What is worse than reading or writing them is living them. There is, I am convinced, nothing worse than living day to day in the coffins of Satan's lies. We all have those days where we feel there is no escape; the bad day just keeps getting worse. Still, there is nothing as tiring as living day after day in a pit that we believe we will never break free from, in a pit we were led to believe would bring us relief, all the while finding only more pain and desperation. We feel there is no escape, there is no hope, this darkness is too deep and we are too far gone. Besides, we've handed Satan the hammer and the nails and told him to have at it, lock us in as many coffins as he wants, because we are done trying to fight him. What is one more coffin? This last lie that he sells women digs deep into our hearts. It is the final nail in the final coffin because once we buy into this lie, once we believe that we are unworthy, we wave our white flag and give up all together. When we give up believing that we are worth anything we also give up hope. If we have no worth then there is no reason to believe anyone could ever see us, search for us, pursue us, love us, or find us worthy of any good thing. In order to expose this final lie of Satan's we must come to understand how he seals us in this coffin or else we shall surrender to this coffin just as easily as we have to the others.

Elyse Fitzpatrick writes,

> "If you belong to Jesus today, your enemy, Satan has two goals: to remind you of your sin and to accuse you continually before God. Satan takes perverse pleasure in reminding you over and over again of your failures...He does this so that you will not love your Savior or have the faith to obey him."[5]

The lies have to be exposed. Satan must not win. Satan cannot win. He will try to remind you over and over of your sins and of your past. He will remind you that you are unseen, unsought, and unpursued. He will remind you so that you don't think God can love you through, and even in spite of your past. He will remind you of your sin so that you won't love God, nor will you allow God to shower you in His love. Satan will remind you of your past so that he can lock you in another coffin, laughing all the while.

Knee Deep in Lies

We have already had our hearts neatly locked away in the coffins of Unseen, Unsought, and Unpursued, yet we still hurt. We still hunger for more because the pain, as Satan told us it would, hasn't actually gone away. We are begging for relief and if we aren't careful who we beg for relief from, then we won't ever be happy with what we get. Sometimes we don't even really realize who we are begging. We turn to the world. We turn to our fathers. We turn to our friends. We turn to our mothers, our bosses, our boyfriends, fiancés, and husbands. We turn left, right, up, and down. We turn in every direction begging for someone to answer the question that is burning in our hearts, *"Am I worthy?"* Am I

---

[5] Fitzpatrick, Elyse. "Silencing the Accuser." *Comforts from the Cross: Celebrating the Gospel One Day at a Time*. Wheaton, IL: Crossway, 2009.

worthy of being noticed, of being sought after, of being pursued, of being loved, cherished, appreciated? Time and time again the world answers us, "as you are, you are unworthy."

Maybe you are blessed with a wonderful family who you actually think is normal; you have friends who love and care about you; you have a man in your life that honors you and respects you. If all of that is true, then one of two things is also true about you: life wasn't always that way or you live in a bubble. Life isn't perfect and it hasn't been since the Fall. Life is messy and filled with disappointments, heartbreaks and pain. I've heard it said many times that to live is to suffer. Take a look outside your window (or your bubble) and you'll see exactly what I'm talking about. Homes are broken, hearts are torn apart, families are breaking at the cracks, pre-teens are pregnant, STDs are running rampant, husbands and wives are divorcing, and the list goes on. We are a broken people. It only makes sense then that we are easily led further astray by Satan and his lies. Like attracts like, remember? We are broken and so is Satan. No wonder we fall so easily into his pit of lies. Why do you think so many people suffer from athazagoraphobia, the fear of being forgotten? We feel unseen and we fear, intensely so, that we will never be remembered. We fall into Satan's pit of lies and we keep falling. One fear leads to another, one coffin leads to another and another and another. "Rest assured," Satan whispers, "we have reached the last one. This is the final stop, the end of the line. There is no turning back now."

The world screams Satan's lies at us, over and over again. It continually tells us that as we are, we are simply unworthy. You must change. You aren't good enough. You aren't pretty enough. You aren't slutty enough. You are too prudish. You are too fat. Too skinny. You hair is too long. Your shade of blonde is disgusting (who came up with dishwater blonde anyway?). Your nose is too big. Your thighs are like tree trunks. Your car isn't fast enough, new enough, or fancy enough. Your house is too small, too old, too outdated. Your school is lame. You'll never amount to anything. You need more make-up. You need to wear this perfume if you ever even hope to get a date. If you don't know how to do this move, you'll never get to second base. If you can't do x, y, or z then you will be a terrible lover. You aren't cool unless you have a tattoo. Or ten. Or an arm full of them. Smoking makes you look cooler. Smoking pot makes you look even cooler. Smoking pot while drinking is the coolest you could get. You aren't good enough as you are. You must buy all these products and wear these designer clothes, fit in with the popular crowd, drive a nice, brand new car, speed and never get caught, date the star of the football team, party like it is your job, maintain perfect grades and then maybe, just maybe you will be worthy. If you are lucky.

    Do you get it yet? Are you laughing? Sure, when we see the lies written on a page they look silly, laughable even. But deep down I can almost bet that you've bought into at least one of those lies. I know I have. They keep coming back and haunting us because Satan hasn't yet won, his mission is not yet complete. Perhaps worse, I can almost guarantee you've said or thought at least one of those lies about someone you know. I've done that too, more times than I would care to count, much less admit to. We perpetuate Satan's lies; we want to drag others down with us.

If we are unworthy as we are, then everyone else must also be unworthy as they are. Drive down any city street and look at the billboards. Does a single one of them make you believe that you, *exactly as you are*, are worthy? Watch five minutes of commercials on TV and you'll be sold ten different products that will make you better than you are now, they will make your life easier, and they'll make it easier for you to get a date because once again, you simply aren't worthy. The world screams it over and over again and because we have so easily been locked in these other coffins, we begin to buy into this final lie: Unworthy.

Unworthy of What?

If we are going to believe this lie, if we are going to be sealed in this final coffin, we must buy into all of the lie in its entirety. It is not enough for Satan to lead us to believe that we are unworthy of love, or hope, or joy, or happiness, or peace, or prosperity, or wealth, or salvation. We must believe that we are unworthy of *all* of those things. How does he get us to believe that we are truly unworthy of all of those things? Remember that slippery slope? We have already been sliding down it with each coffin. Once we get down to this point, once we reach this level of desolation and desperation it becomes easy for Satan to convince us one by one that we are unworthy of anything remotely resembling happiness, goodness or salvation. If you asked the average girl on the street how she would feel if you called her unworthy she would probably say that it made her feel sad or lonely. However, if you asked a girl that who is already sad and depressed she would probably say that it feels like truth to her. We believe we are no longer worthy of good things, much less salvation. After all, we sold part of our soul for those designer clothes so we could attract the eye of that cute guy. Then we sold another part of our soul so that he would search for us. We sold yet another part so he would at least appear to pursue us. Then we gave away even more of our souls the first time we hooked up with a guy or the first time we slept with him. Finally, we gave away the last bits of our soul with each new guy we hooked up with or slept with, especially if we didn't know them, care about them, or even know their names. If we could use people like that then why should we be redeemed? Why should we deserve happiness, peace, joy, or love? If we are capable of such deception and back-stabbing then why should we be prosperous or wealthy? We are fundamentally unworthy. We are horrid, sinful people who only know how to sin and use and step on others. We deserve everything we have coming to us, and nothing headed our way is good. We can't possibly be worthy of mercy. Justice is knocking on our doors (or rather our coffins) and we feel we have no right, no place, and no need to hope for mercy. We have been condemned. We have damned ourselves. We are unworthy. Period.

Twisted Words

"Christ Jesus came into the world to save sinners. Of these I am the foremost." – 1 Timothy 1:15

"For I am the least of the apostles, who am not worthy…" – 1 Corinthians 15:9[6]

---

[6] Rheims New Testament.

Whenever I think about Saint Paul, these are two of the first verses that come to my mind. There is not a Christian denomination I know of that does not revere or honor Saint Paul. We acknowledge Paul to be a great sinner and he even goes so far as to call himself the greatest sinner. Yet he says he is the least of the apostles and he is unworthy. My word, if Saint Paul is unworthy then what hope do the rest of us have? Even if I don't think of myself as the greatest sinner on Earth, I have to acknowledge that Saint Paul was one amazing, holy man. Sure, he didn't start out that way, but his missions spread the Gospel message farther and wider than any could have imagined. His letters not only make up nearly half of the New Testament, but they have shaped, and continue to shape theology in a way unmatched by any one of the other apostles. Still, he believes himself unworthy. Too often I've found it easy to twist his words to keep myself in a pit of sadness and depression. If Saint Paul is unworthy then I too, who am far less holy than he, must also be unworthy.

I don't just twist the words of Saint Paul, and I'm willing to bet we all twist more words than those of Scripture. I can't tell you how many times someone has said to me something along the lines of, "I really like how you phrased this sentence, but that whole paragraph after that needs to go, it makes no sense" but all I hear is, "That whole paragraph is horrid. Why do you even bother writing anything?" Other times the statements go like this, "That shirt is really cute, but your hair is all over the place today!" and I hear, "That haircut you just got is awful and makes you look like a boy." Locked in the coffins we've already been confined to, we being to doubt what is true. We don't find the silver lining in life anymore. We begin to embrace the darkness, thus making it even easier for Satan to convince us that we are unworthy. We twist the words of Scripture and we twist the words of others so that we no longer hear any positive message, we only hear people tearing us down.

My mom often tells me that I seek advice from people who I know will tell me what I want to hear. It is only natural and we all do it. When I want someone to tell me that I should write a book I know in my heart who will encourage me and who will not (when I started this project I only told the select few who I knew would encourage and support me). When I am annoyed with one of my friends I know which other friends I can talk to about it who will have my back and take my side, no matter what, even if I'm the one in the wrong. Call it confirmation bias; we seek validation of our own thoughts from those who are most likely to validate them. You wouldn't go to your parish priest if you wanted someone to tell you that partying, getting drunk and sleeping around was normal behavior. You wouldn't seek spiritual advice from the guy you hooked-up with last night. We seek advice from the sources most likely to validate us, so it is not a huge leap that once we are sliding down the slippery slope of Satan's lies we only hear more disappointment, discouragement, and desolation. We hear what we have come to believe we already are: unseen, unsought, unpursued, and fundamentally unworthy.

Entrenched and Believing

We own the lies, we make them our own. This process is only natural. If we are told something enough times, or if we tell ourselves something enough times, we begin to believe it is true. If a parent tells their child over and over again that they will pass their math test, the child will begin to believe that they will pass the math test. Similarly, if that same parent told their child that when they were young they failed math, so the child will probably fail math too, the child will more than likely believe that he or she is doomed to fail math. Scientists and psychologists call this the placebo effect. If we believe we are being given medicine (or in this case lies) that will affect us one way or the other, that result often happens. The mind is more powerful than we often give it credit for.

The same is true of the things we tell ourselves. If we wake up in the morning and stub our toe getting out of bed, we may begin to think that we are going to have a bad day. What we believe will happen usually ends up happening. We look for all the bad things in the day. However, the opposite is also true, if we are faced with a stressful, horrible, daunting situation and we continue to assure ourselves that it won't be as bad as we imagine it to be, slowly we begin to believe we can get through it. We believe what we are told, or what we tell ourselves. We naturally look for things to confirm what we already think, either that life is good or that life is bad, either that we are worthy or that we are unworthy.

The lies are beat into our heads and our hearts and they make their home within our souls. In many ways these lies are similar to trenches often used in warfare. Troops dig their way into the ground and hide out in the trenches. In order to keep troops safe from incoming bullets and enemy fire, the trenches must be dug very deep into the ground. The deeper the trenches, the safer the troops were from enemy fire. If the trench was shallow troops risked poking their heads or limbs up and being shot. Troops dug trenches so deep that they could stand up in them comfortably. Satan's lies work in the same way. The deeper he buries his lies in our hearts, the safer the lies are and the safer he is. If he only buried his lies knee-deep in our hearts he would risk attack from his enemy (God) and his defense would be blown. So he tells us more lies, locks us in more coffins and entrenches his lies on our hearts. These lies are entrenched so deeply that if we aren't careful, we too join in the battle, and defend Satan. When we begin to defend Satan, we give him room to dig his trenches even deeper in our hearts, often to disastrous ends.

The Tragic, Bitter End

To write this chapter without touching on the bitter end of this lie (and all the lies of Satan) would be a terrible oversight. All too often I've seen first-hand what believing in these lies can and will do to a person. When we believe that we are unworthy, when we accept that such a state of life is the only state of life, we are left without hope. Void of hope too many people are driven to hopeless, permanent choices.

My junior year in high school was a tragic example of what can happen when we believe we are unworthy. That year alone we had twelve deaths in our high school. Mind you, I went to a fairly sizeable high school of about 2,500 students. Nine of those deaths were suicide. The first one was the week after homecoming, and the last one was the day before graduation that year. It wasn't just one class, one week, or one common denominator across the board that led to so many suicides. I can't tell you how many times I've reflected on the tragedy of that year, of the lives cut short and all that those people could have accomplished in their lifetimes. While I didn't know all of the people who died that year, I knew a number of them, to varying degrees. I can't tell you why any one of them committed suicide. I'm fairly sure that the reasons they chose to end their lives are as numerous as the stars in the sky. Each person had his/her own reasons – right, wrong, or otherwise – at least I believe they did because the alternative only makes the tragedy that much more depressing. We can guess and have our theories, but I can't tell you in their heart of hearts why they did it. I can tell you that I wish they were all still here today. There isn't a June 1st that rolls around without me stopping to take notice that it has been another year since one of my friends, whom I had known since middle school, took her own life. I can remember that day as though it was yesterday, from the moment I left the house and I told my mom that when I came home that day I would forever be a different person, to laying my head down and crying myself to sleep that night. I hope and pray that I will get to see her again someday. I hope and pray that somehow, some way, something good can come from her death; some small ray of hope could come out of such a tragic end. Even as I write this, one of my friends from college is missing and it is believed that he, too, committed suicide. There are simply no words to describe the gravity of such a tragedy. It breaks my heart to know that anyone could reach a point where they believe they are unworthy and that life simply isn't worth living. I pray that God can make sense out of their deaths and I pray that He can bring about good in the face of such heartbreak. To make a point out of their deaths would be insensitive, but I hope that we can learn something from them, or else we risk their lives and their deaths being meaningless and unworthy forever. Satan sells us lies, and sometimes when we buy into enough coffins the last one we buy into won't be metaphorical, it will be literal. We must, we must, we must expose the lies.

Passionately Hated and Passionately Loved

No matter how far into Satan's trenches you have fallen, no matter how far you have descended into his pit of lies, no matter how many sins you've fallen prey to, it is never too late to bring God's light into the darkness. Corrie ten Boom and her family hid Jews in their house during World War II. When the Nazis invaded her home country of the Netherlands the number of Jews the ten Booms hid increased. Eventually the ten Booms' secret room was discovered and the family was sent to concentration camps. Corrie's father died ten days after arriving at the Scheveningen prison. Corrie's sister, Nollie, her brother, Willem, and her nephew, Peter, were later released. However, Corrie and her other sister, Betsie, were passed between concentration camps. Before Betsie died she told Corrie, "There is no pit so deep that God's love is not deeper still."[7] Betsie told Corrie that she believed they would be free by the end of the year. Betsie died on December 16th, 1944. Corrie was released on New Year's Eve in 1944.

It would be hard to argue that Corrie had not descended into the pits of hell in those concentration camps, especially with the loss of her sister and her father. Corrie later learned that her

---

[7] Ten Boom, Corrie, John L. Sherrill, and Elizabeth Sherrill. *The Hiding Place*. Washington Depot, CT: Chosen, 1971.

release had been due to a clerical error, and that the women prisoners her age in the camp from which she was released were killed one week after her release. In the movie based on her autobiography, *The Hiding Place*, Corrie narrates and says of her release that "God does not have problems. Only plans."[8] Corrie went on to travel and tell the world of God's goodness and His love. She took her sister's words to heart and continually preached the message that "no matter how deep our darkness, He is deeper still."[9] There is no pit of lies, no trench so deep that God cannot reach into it and ransom our hearts. Hope is never gone. Corrie promised her sister that she would share their story with the world. Coming out of the concentration camps fatherless and having watched her sister die, Corrie still managed to hold on to hope. She knew that "with Jesus, even in our darkest moments, the best remains and the very best will be."[10]

If we are to be people who live in and cling to hope, we must expose the lies that Satan continues to tell women, and for that matter, to all of God's children. We close the ears of our hearts off to Satan and his countless tricks, unending deception and deadly lies. Stasi Eldredge explains better than I when she writes,

> "You won't really understand your life as a woman until you understand this:

---

[8] *The Hiding Place*. Dir. James F. Collier. Perf. Julie Harris and Jeannette Clift. World Wide Pictures, 1975. Transcript.

[9] Ibid.

[10] Ibid.

You are passionately loved by the God of the universe.

You are passionately hated by His Enemy.

And so, dear heart, it is time for your restoration. For there is One greater than your Enemy. One who has sought you out from the beginning of time. He has come to heal your broken heart and restore your feminine soul."[11]

It is time to be restored. It is time to break free of the coffins. It is time to be seen, to be sought after, to be pursued, and to be found worthy. There is One greater than these lies. There is One greater than your deepest darkness. Are you ready to meet Him? Are you ready to be healed by Him? Are you ready to be loved by Him? Come, let us seek His warm, compassionate, loving, forgiving, and merciful Heart.

---

[11] Eldredge, John, and Stasi Eldredge. "A Special Hatred." *Captivating*. Nashville, TN: Thomas Nelson, 2005. 91.

The Triumph of Love

"The only thing necessary for the triumph of evil is for good men to do nothing." – Edmund Burke

"Sometimes the things that may or may not be true are the things [we] need to believe in the most. That people are basically good; that honor, courage, and virtue mean everything; that power and money, money and power mean nothing; that good always triumphs over evil; and I want you to remember this, that love... true love never dies." – Uncle Hub in *Secondhand Lions*

Help Me...

"Accepting the reality of our broken, flawed lives is the beginning...because we let go of seeking perfection and, instead, seek God, the one who is present in the tangledness of our lives."
– Mike Yaconelli

We all worship and honor something. Some worship and honor money, others a good job, others a great spouse and wonderful children. Still others worship and honor God and they seek Him with their whole hearts. What do you worship? What do you honor? Are you seeking the God who is present in all of the messiness of this life, or are you still following the Father of Lies, who only makes the messiness worse, darker, and more depressing? Are you willing to let go of seeking to make your life perfect, to let go of the lies and accept your broken reality? If you are then this is where the real journey begins. This is where the rubber meets the road. This is where we find out what we are made of. This is also where, if we are willing, we discover the unending majesty, power, and love of God. If we accept our brokenness, if we bring all of the broken pieces to God, then the real work begins as we seek Him, who is Perfection, instead of following and seeking the empty promises of Satan.

Over and over again in Scripture God is referred to as the potter, and we, His people, are the clay in His hands. Every time I look at a clay pot it makes me think of God and how much I connect with the image of God as the potter and us as the clay. We are being formed. I once interviewed with the National Evangelization Team (NET) and during the interview weekend there was an amazing talk about the Potter and the clay. We sat and listened as the speaker told us that we are like clay in the Potter's hands. We sat in this nice, quiet, and quaint chapel when all of a sudden, seemingly out of nowhere, the speaker threw the clay pot he was using for the visual on the ground, smashing it into countless pieces. We all sat in stunned silence until the speaker continued and explained that we are like that pot and we get smashed when we sin, and when we buy into Satan's lies. The only way for us to be fixed is for us to take all of the broken pieces, no matter how small or big, back to God.

Jesus, in fact, already paid the price for our broken clay pots. When Judas realized what he had done after he betrayed Jesus, he tried to return the money to the chief priests. Not wanting to deposit the money into the treasury because it was now considered blood money, the chief priests used the money to buy "the potter's field."[1] The potter's field was the place where potters would throw away their broken, damaged, or imperfect pots. The field was full of bits and pieces of clay that no longer seemed to have any use. Jesus' life paid for that field, He paid the price for our brokenness in hopes that we would be healed and learn to bring all of our brokenness to Him. After the talk was over we were invited to take a piece of the broken pot as a reminder of our own brokenness and God's healing touch. The shard of that pot that I took is in my Bible case and it reminds me that even when I'm broken, He still holds and loves me.

There was another piece to that weekend, a phrase that has always resonated in my heart, "You can't give what you don't have." I can't give you bread if I didn't go to the store to buy any. I

---

[1] Matthew 27:3-10

can't give the homeless man on the street any money if I don't carry cash. I can't give you love if I'm not being loved and shown what love is. You can't give what you don't have. We can't give if we aren't receiving, and we can't feed others if we aren't being fed ourselves. So where can we be fed? We are fed in and because of Jesus.

The Most Common Phrase

A few years ago I went on what I, and many of my friends before me, called a dating fast. We defined a dating fast as a period of time that a person takes, in my case it was three months, where they abstain from dating to focus more intentionally on their relationship with God. My dating fast was one of the best things I have ever experienced, not only for me, but for my future relationships, and more importantly for my relationship with Jesus. For me, I had been in a few relationships that ended (some better than others) and I was growing really tired of the dating scene. My heart was hurt and confused and I needed a break from it all, so I prayed about it and decided to go on a dating fast. During that time I also decided to start keeping a prayer journal. Over the course of my life I had started many, many journals and wrote in them for no more than two weeks – usually inconsistently – before throwing the whole project out the window (not literally of course, I didn't want anyone to find and read my journals). When I started my dating fast I committed to journaling every single day about what God was putting on my heart and what I was learning.

At the end of the three months it just so happened that I was on vacation and had gone to visit Mepkin Abbey, a Trappist monastery in South Carolina, and easily one of my favorite places to visit. As soon as you drive onto the monks' property you are greeted by a long road overshadowed by towering trees covered in Spanish moss and gorgeous, blooming flowers of endless shades of pink, purple, yellow, and red. It is a place I love to visit because it is so peaceful and relaxing, so it was the perfect place to be as my dating fast drew to a close. I decided to re-read my journal, cover to cover, before the sun went down. I sat on a beautiful edge of the property, surrounded by palm trees and overlooking a beautiful lagoon, and I began to read all of what God had put in my heart in three months' time. The sun slowly began to fade and set over the lagoon and the colors of that sunset are forever burned in my mind. The cool night air began to set in, and though I didn't finish reading the whole journal before sunset – I had written a lot in those three months – one phrase popped up time and time again: "Help me…" Re-reading my journal taught me how much I had come to, and needed to come to, a complete dependence on God. Whether I was praying for Him to help me not excessively flirt with guys, or increase my prayer life, or the depths of my prayers, I was and am constantly praying for His help in whatever I do. Like a fish out of water, I came to realize that without Him I am nothing. Even if you opened up any one of my more recent journals you will still find the pages littered with "help me" or phrases similar to it. The more I pray for His help, the more I find myself truly needing it. Without His help I am a ship lost at sea.

    I need help. I've never been one to easily admit that. As a child I hated asking for help in school because I didn't want the teacher or my peers to think that I was stupid. I would rather have failed a test than asked for help. It took me a long time before I ever asked for help in school or with anything, but once I did I found that no one thought I was stupid, and most people were eager to help me learn and grow. Father Chris Kirchgessner, O.S.B., taught that we sin, not because we are human, but because we are being less than we were created to be. All too often in my life I have been less than I was created to be, which is exactly why I need His help. I can't give what I don't have, and God is the easiest, most accessible source of every good thing in the universe. If I have any hope of being all that I was created to be, then I need His help, and I need His grace.

KT Tunstall sings in "Black Horse and a Cherry Tree" that our hearts know us better than we even know ourselves, so why not let our hearts do all the talking? When we pray, this is the way that we should pray, from our hearts. Our hearts know us better than we know ourselves. I'm not referring to the heart beating in your chest because that doesn't intuitively know much of anything about us, except for how to beat and pump blood (not that we aren't thankful for that). When I refer to the heart in this sense I am speaking of the place where our desires, our fears, our hopes, and our aspirations reside. Perhaps more accurately the heart is the dwelling place of God, the place where He seeks to make His home within us.[2] If God truly dwells in our hearts then it makes sense that our hearts know us better than we know ourselves, because God knows us better than we know ourselves. When I journal I try to let my heart do all the talking, which is why time and time again I find myself writing "Help me", because my heart

---

[2] CCC2517, 2563

knows how much I need His help and strength to get me through the trials of this life. Would we rather our hearts, the dwelling place of God, do all the talking, or our heads? Our heads can far too easily be led astray by the latest fads or the lies Satan tells us, but it is our heart that always calls us home and reminds of what we truly desire, thus saving us from eternally being locked inside coffins.

Saint Irenaeus is credited with saying that "The glory of God is man fully alive." For me, being fully alive means living from my heart. I feel most fully alive when I'm driving in the mountains, when I'm hiking, and when I'm sitting and enjoying the beauty of creation. I feel alive when I'm at Mass, and I feel alive when I finish a true and honest confession. I feel alive when I take time out of a hectic day to just sit in a Eucharistic Adoration chapel and rest in the arms of the Lord. When I'm not living from my heart I find that I am afraid and scared of the days to come and I'm uncertain about anything and everything. Fear comes from the head. Courage, however, comes from the heart. The word courage comes from the French word "coeur" which means "heart". Courage is not the absence of fear, it is the ability to look fear in the face and say, "I acknowledge that you are here, but you will not defeat me." Courage comes from the place where God dwells, and it gives us the ability to stand up instead of withering away behind fear. The virtue of courage gives us the strength to admit that, though we are not strong enough to overcome all of life's challenges on our own, there is still hope. Because courage comes from the heart it most readily asks for help from the One who dwells within it: God Himself. Courage gives us the grace to beg of God, "Help me, I need Your love, Your strength, Your wisdom, and Your grace to face the challenges before me." Courage says, "I can't do this without You," whereas pride and fear say, "I can do this on my own, I don't need You. I'd rather be crippled by fear than accept help."

Pride told me that people would think I was stupid if I asked for help in school. Courage told pride to go away because there was something bigger at stake, and isn't there always something bigger than pride at stake? Isn't our eternal life at stake? Courage takes the bigger step in asking for help and courage wins the day because, as Scripture says, "If God is for us, who can be against us?"[3]

The Cries of the Psalms

The prophet Jeremiah spends a lot of his writing lamenting various hardships and difficulties in his life and in the lives of those around him. However, I think he could not have written truer words than these, "More tortuous than all else is the human heart, beyond remedy; who can understand it? I, the Lord, alone probe the mind and test the heart."[4] Think about that. Nothing in the entire world is more complex, more full of twists and turns, than the human heart. Nothing is less straightforward than the human heart. Wouldn't you agree? Perhaps men might not think this about their own hearts, but just about every woman I know would agree, there is nothing so confusing and complex as the human heart. I'm also willing to bet that men would agree that the heart of a woman is the most complicated thing on the planet. Everything

---

[3] Romans 8:31.

[4] Jeremiah 17:9-10a.

is held within our hearts: our hopes, our dreams, our fears, our hurts, everything. No wonder it is so complex! Jeremiah even says that it is beyond remedy and he wonders who could possibly understand it. Who on earth could ever understand the twists and turns of the human heart? No one. Not yet, anyway. The only one Jeremiah knew of (because Jeremiah lived before Jesus was born) who could understand the human heart was the One who created it. God *alone* probes the mind and tests the heart; He understands the never ending maze of our hearts. Only God knows the remedy for the complexities of the human heart because, as Saint Augustine famously wrote, our hearts are made for God and they are restless until they rest in Him, and Him alone.

Even though we know that God is the only One who can truly understand our hearts, we still find ourselves begging for Him to come, for Him to rescue us. We forget that He is with us always.[5] Our hearts know what they want: God. Our hearts want to be understood and acknowledged. Our hearts want to be seen, to be sought after, to be pursued, and to be found worthy. As Blaise Pascal is credited with saying, "The heart has reasons which reason knows nothing of." There may be no logical reason for wanting God, for needing Him, but the heart knows what and who it was made for, and the heart longs for its Creator like a child longs for its mother. This longing is as old as time. We find these desires over and over again in Scripture, but especially in the Psalms. In Psalm 6 King David writes, "In utter terror is my soul – and you, Lord, how long…? Turn, Lord, save my life; in your

---

[5] Matthew 28:20

mercy rescue me."[6] How long until You answer my prayer Lord? We sit, we wait, we wonder. We plead with God to turn and look at us, we plead with Him to save our life, and to rescue us. No matter who you are I can guarantee there has been a time in your life where you wanted to be rescued. Maybe it was an awkward situation at school, maybe your parents were fighting, maybe you got busted for breaking curfew, maybe you had your heart broken, but you wanted to be rescued. There have been more than a few times in my life when I have literally and figuratively cried out to God for Him to rescue me. I waited in silence hoping the heavens would open up and God would speak some comforting words into my heart; I waited hoping that He would rescue me. We wonder how long it will be until God answers us, until God hears us and saves us.

I've had a number of times in my life when I wished that God would have turned and rescued me. When I was thirteen my step-grandfather, Papa, died of a heart attack. It was gut-wrenching and unexpected, and hit me like a ton of bricks. Two days later my great aunt died. Two months later my great-grandma came to visit for my dad's fortieth birthday party. She contracted meningitis and was rushed to the hospital where she died in a matter of hours. Three months, three deaths. I wanted nothing more than for God to save me from this seemingly unending line of deaths. It got to a point where I woke up in the morning wondering if I could make it through the day without having another family member die. "And you, Lord, how long…?" were words my heart would have easily related to, had I been

---

[6] v. 4-5

aware of them at the time. I hungered for peace and for an end to the pain, but it never really seemed to come. I hungered and yet I felt hurt still, and I didn't trust that He would feed my hunger; I couldn't see why God would allow such anguish in my life. I couldn't see, at least not then, that I was hungry for someone who would never leave me, never die, and never purposely break my heart. I was hungry for God.

The Psalms go on about the desire to be rescued, the desire to be understood, and the desire to be pursued. "My God, my God, why have you abandoned me? Why so far from my call for help, from my cries of anguish? My God, I call by day, but you do not answer; by night, but I have no relief."[7] We long for God. "As the deer longs for streams of water, so my soul longs for you, O God. My being thirsts for God, the living God. When can I go and see the face of God?"[8] Reading those words I can't help but feel the psalmists' struggles and desires. Their words tug at my heartstrings and I wish that I could answer their prayers. We hunger and thirst for God. The cry to be rescued continues to this day. We not only want to know, we feel that we need to know, to know God, and to be rescued. We hear this pleading in countless songs and books today. We want to see His face, we want to be freed from the sufferings and the anguish of this life, and we know that the only way out, the only way through our struggles, is found in God. King David knows this as he writes in Psalm 31, "You are my rock and my fortress; for your name's sake lead and guide me. Free me from the net they have set for me, for you are my refuge."[9]

---

[7] Psalm 22:1-2

[8] Psalm 42:1-2

God alone is our hope and our salvation, so we continually call out to Him for help and courage because we know that only He can save us. Only God can understand our hearts and minds, and only He can lead us by still waters into His mercy.

The cry to be close to God, to have Him come and rescue us, isn't going away anytime soon. Think of the songs you hear on the radio; don't most of them sing about the desire to be understood, whether it is by God, your boyfriend, your best friend, your mother, or whoever? Kari Jobe sings about this same desire in her song, "Run To You (I Need You)". We can never get enough of God. We come alive in His presence, so it is no wonder that we run to Him, and that we long for Him. Because we come alive in His presence we continue to run to Him, we need Him to help us, and we need Him to heal us. We need Him to free us.

We Are Not Alone

When a rash of my relatives died when I was thirteen, I began to feel as though I was alone. Please don't misunderstand me, I was and am incredibly grateful for the relatives that are still living, but nonetheless I started to feel alone. I didn't realize that I was hungering for God. Instead, I railed against Him because He took my family members from me; I believed that He caused me to experience loneliness. Instead of clinging to Him, to the God who would never leave me, I turned my back on Him. I hated Him for causing, or at least allowing, such pain and suffering to enter my life, and I could not and would not allow myself to worship, much less love a God who seemed to show me so little love and

---

[9] v. 4-5

compassion in return. It took a number of years for me to see that even though I had left God, He had never left me. It took a long time for me to face God, and to admit that I really was hungry, famished even, for His love. I reached a point in my life when I couldn't do things alone. I'm not talking about those girls who could never seem to be able to go to the bathroom alone, I mean that I found it really difficult to process events and situations alone. I couldn't face the nine suicides during my junior year in high school without Him. I needed some higher power, someone wiser than myself, to guide me through what lay before me. I had to believe there was some greater purpose; I had to believe there was more to life than this existence. I needed something firm and constant to cling to. I had finally, after years of searching, come to a point where I truly believed that I am not alone, ever. It is not as though we all have some creepy stalker, it means that even in our darkest hours, He is there with us.

Not only is God with us, He goes before us. The author of Deuteronomy writes, "It is the Lord who marches before you; he will be with you and will never fail you or forsake you. So do not fear or be dismayed."[10] The Lord doesn't just walk before you, He doesn't skip before you, He *marches* before you. What a powerful image that conjures. The God of the universe, the creator of all that is good, marches before you and guards your heart. He marches and protects us. This, as we know all too well, does not necessarily mean He will shield us from all of the pain and suffering of this life, but He will go before us. Think of battle strategies, would you really want to be the one on the front lines?

---

[10] Dt. 31:8

Isn't it safer to be holding up the rear? With God, He is always on the front lines. I shudder to think how miserable life would be if God did not march before us. He marches before us so that we can be safer. God marching before us doesn't mean we won't see battle. He knows we will, but it does mean that the injuries won't be as life-threatening, and we will see less combat than if God did not march before us.

We can't do this alone; alone we perish. Alone we are locked in coffins with no hope of ever escaping. Alone our hearts break. Together we triumph, which is exactly why we are invited to turn to the God who has already overcome every temptation of this life. Matt Maher sings in his song, "Remembrance", that when we look upon Christ we see that Christ has overcome every struggle we will ever face. In Christ we understand that there is no one too lost to be saved, and that there is no one too ashamed or broken to be welcomed by God. All are welcomed because we need each other; we need fellowship and constant reminders that He alone is the source of all the goodness our hearts long for. Jesus knew, and told His apostles and followers over and over again, that in this world we will face troubles. If we love Him then the world will hate us. We will be mocked and despised for loving Him. Jesus told His apostles, "I have told you this so that you may not fall away. They will expel you from the synagogues; in fact, the hour is coming when everyone who kills you will think they are offering worship to God...I have told you this so that when their hour comes you may remember that I told you."[11] He did not want us to turn or fall away from Him. He knew that hatred and

---

[11] John 16:1-2, 4

persecution were coming, we aren't without warning. He knew that Satan would come at us with his lies and his coffins, seeking to lock us away in them forever. We also aren't without hope. Jesus reminds His apostles and He reminds us, "I am not alone, because the Father is with me. I have told you this so that you might have peace in me. In the world you will have trouble, but take courage, I have conquered the world."[12] Jesus was never alone and neither are we. He has told us that there will be trouble, not to frighten us, but to invite us to find peace in Him. He sent us the Advocate, the Holy Spirit, so that we would never be alone, even once Jesus had ascended into Heaven. He invites us to take courage, to take heart, to hold on to the dwelling place of God, and to invite God to dwell more richly within us. Jesus has conquered the world. God marches before us always. Take heart, dear friends. Jesus has triumphed over the world and He invites you into His Father's heart to be healed so that, with Him by our sides, we too may conquer the lies of the world and be found worthy.

---

[12] John 16:33

Monkey Bars

"Getting over a painful experience is much like crossing monkey bars: You have to let go at some point in order to move forward."
– C.S. Lewis

God knows that there have been hundreds of thousands of books written on suffering. There are books about why we suffer, how to avoid suffering, how to deal with suffering, and probably even how to make others suffer. I daresay there are not enough good books out there on moving forward from pain and suffering. It isn't enough to move on from pain and suffering, nor is it enough to simply survive suffering. I refuse to believe that suffering is something we must simply endure, like a bad root canal. God, in His loving mercy, wants to *heal* us through and from our sufferings. Suffering will exist, it has since The Fall. He won't take it from us, but He can and will heal our hurts. He wants us to get to Heaven with unbroken hearts and pearly white souls. As Isaiah the prophet tells us, the Lord wants us to be healed and cleaned, "Come now, let us set things right, says the Lord: Though your sins be like scarlet, they may become white as snow; though they be crimson red, they may become white as wool."[1]

Much like C.S. Lewis once wrote, we have to let go of the monkey bars in order to move forward. We need healing, and it is there for us in the arms of Christ. We need to move forward or we risk sliding backwards and returning to the coffins that once enslaved us. Lewis, however, had it perfectly right when he wrote that "At some point" we have to let go. God gives us the free will to

---

[1] Isaiah 1:18

determine when that point is. There is no handbook that says: 23 days after someone dies you have to let go. Seventy-three hours after a break up you must stop crying about it. Five days after your best friend lied to you, you must forgive her. Six weeks after you quit your job you have to go back and tell your boss what a nice person you think he or she is, no matter how they wronged you. Four and a half days after your boyfriend cheats on you, you should forgive him, and the girl he cheated on you with. Such a rulebook or handbook would be insane. Jesus tells Peter that we are to forgive "not seven times, but seventy-seven times."[2] Jesus never says, "You must forgive your brother today." He tells us that we are to forgive, not necessarily when to forgive. C.S. Lewis says much the same thing about our painful life experiences, we have to let go, but he doesn't try to tell us when to let go. That decision remains ours.

Broken and Beautiful

Everyone has those days when you are driving down the road and suddenly a song comes on the radio and it hits you upside the head. I've had more of these days than I can count. There was one day and song in particular that I actually pulled my car over on the freeway because I began to cry so deeply that I couldn't keep driving.

For months I had been in a relationship with a guy and things had been really rough. We had struggled a lot with remaining pure and chaste. When I say we struggled, I mean we also failed. A lot. It got to me and it ate away at my heart, it ate

---

[2] Matthew 18:22

away at the place that God was and is seeking to make His home. God, who always seeks to dwell in my heart, knew the aches and pains of my heart and I believe He sent this song just for me on that day. Every time I've heard this song since then I think back to the first time I heard it and was overcome with healing tears. In a beautiful acoustic sound the words of "Come As You Are" by Pocket Full of Rocks rang out over the radio waves declaring that God is not mad at us. He's not disappointed in us either. In fact, His grace is greater than any and all of the wrong choices we've ever made. I barely made it through those beginning lines without crying as I pulled my car over to the side of the road. Even now, as I relive the first time I heard the song, tears come to my eyes. I was a broken woman and my heart was crying out, and yet I felt unworthy. I had sinned; I had messed up and fallen short of the woman He created me to be. I was sure He was mad at me, and I was sure that He was disappointed in me. I was absolutely certain that He looked down at me with pity and disappointment at all of my failures and sins. Hearing those words that day gave me the strength to move one monkey bar ahead in my journey towards Heaven. In that moment, crying on the side of the road, I finally began to receive His healing. I began to believe that He wasn't mad at me, nor was He disappointed in me. I trusted, and continue to trust, that His grace is greater than all of my wrong choices, which, at times, have been many. In that car on the side of the road I began to let go of the painful experience of sinning and struggling with my relationship and with chastity, and I began to move toward His healing love. That monkey bar was the first of many, and it hasn't always been an easy road, but I'd rather be moving forward, however painfully, than clinging to the same monkey bar and getting nowhere.

Pocket Full of Rocks continue to sing, reminding us that God is full of mercy and that His kindness is as boundless as the seas. The band invites us to hear God's invitation to come as we are, no matter how broken or ashamed we feel. The invitation from God is to come with our pain and scars and bring it all to Jesus. There are countless amazing songs about being healed by Christ's love, and I often used to wonder why songs along that theme are so numerous. Then one day it hit me: songs about healing are so numerous because we are all in such desperate need of healing. We all need to let go of the monkey bars and move forward. We need to know and believe that we can truly come as we are and be washed in His mercy. He invites us to come to His open arms just as we are, broken and shameful. We bring it all to Him and we find healing and restoration for our broken hearts.

The more I think about it, the more I have come to believe that God loves our emptiness and our brokenness. It has often been said that everyone has a God-sized hole in their hearts. All too often we try to fill that hole with other things, and countless lies, before we come to Him, empty, and beg Him to fill that hole with the only thing it can be filled with. Peter Kreeft writes,

> "The big, blazing, terrible truth about man is that he has a heaven-sized hole in his heart, and nothing else can fill it. We pass our lives trying to fill the Grand Canyon with marbles. As Augustine said, 'Thou hast made us for thyself, and our hearts are restless until they rest in thee.'"[3]

Matt Maher sings about this emptiness in his song, "Empty and Beautiful". Just the title of that song speaks volumes; it says that even when we are empty, even when we feel lost and alone, still He finds us beautiful. Maher sings about how often we feel that our past haunts us. He sings about how our past can be like a prison in which there is a fight between who we are now and who we used to be. So we hang on to the monkey bar, we hang on to what is familiar, even if it is filled with pain. Letting go and flying into the unknown is far scarier to us than clinging to the pain we have grown so accustomed to. There is a prison, there are coffins all around us, and we are trying to escape. As we seek to escape, to move forward with our lives we often find that there is not just a struggle but an honest to God fight between who we are, who we want to be, and who we have been. Our past won't stop haunting us; it leaves us feeling empty and alone, just as we felt locked in all those coffins. But Maher goes on to sing of how Christ fights the good fight in us, Christ chases us down and helps us finish the race. Jesus keeps the faith in us. Jesus has fought the fight in us, He has already overcome the trials and hardships we face. He finds us as we are, He invites us to come, empty and broken, and He still sees the beauty within us.

Open and Optimistic

Let's face it, we are broken people. Even when God sings to us and tells us that in our brokenness we are still beautiful, we remain broken, unless we do something about it. Archbishop Charles J. Chaput once wrote, "Suffering can bend and break us.

---

[3] Kreeft, Peter. "Heaven." *Heaven*. Ignatius Press. Web.
<http://www.peterkreeft.com/topics/heaven.htm>.

But it can also *break us open* to become the persons God intended us to be. It depends on what we do with the pain. If we offer it back to God, he will use it to do great things in us and through us because suffering is fertile."[4] The pain in our lives is real and we can try to ignore it all we want, but it will still remain. We try to numb it with alcohol or diets or by not thinking about the pain and burying it away, but in the end it simply doesn't work. What happens when you bury a seed? It grows. When we bury our hurts, it is like burying a seed, and given the right conditions, which Satan will do his best to make possible, the original pain will only grow. It will grow roots and make its home in our hearts. However, suffering can also break us open. Suffering can lead us to close our hearts off to others or it can open our hearts to others, so that we can become the person God intends for us to be. If we offer Him the pain instead of burying it, He can and will make it fertile for our benefit and for His glory. He can make beauty come from the ashes. He can make life come from death, and He already has through His Son. If we offer our pain and our suffering back to Him, He blesses it, He accepts it as His own, and He makes it fertile.

My youth minister used to always tell us to "offer it up" when we would complain about anything. As teenagers, naturally, we complained about a lot, so we were quite frequently told to "offer it up". It took me a long time to understand what she meant when she would challenge us in this way. Now I understand that

---

[4] Chaput, Charles J. "God's Covenant Fulfilled in Mary's Fiat." *Archdiocese of Denver*. Denver Catholic Register, 28 Mar. 2001. Web.
<http://www.archden.org/dcr/archive/20010328/2001032801ab.htm>. Empahsis added.

we can offer our sufferings up to God, and that they can be our sacrifices of praise to Him. Our suffering can bring Him glory. Saint Therese of Lisieux once noted, "Sufferings gladly borne for others convert more people than sermons." Our suffering can convert others and can point others to the God who gives us peace even in the most trying times in our lives. Perhaps it is in our sufferings that we are most united to Christ for it is there, deep in our own sufferings, that we are united to His heart as He willingly suffered for us. Perhaps it is in offering up our sufferings that we most clearly understand what love is truly about.

Do you ever remember having a splinter as a kid? Chances are your mom probably had to pull a few out of your hands when you were younger, and chances are that you probably didn't enjoy it. Some moms use really pointy tweezers to get the splinters out. As a kid those pointy tweezers seemed far more painful than the splinter in my hand. However, I knew that if my parents or I left the splinter there it would just get worse over time and cause even more pain. No matter how deeply I knew that, I still dreaded the tweezers. No one really wants someone else digging around in their flesh to pull out some tiny little splinter. The tweezers only increase the pain, but that increased pain is necessary if the splinter is going to be removed in order to avoid additional pain.

The same scenario is true in our relationship with God. C.S. Lewis compares God to a surgeon when he writes,

> "But suppose that what you are up against is a surgeon whose intentions are wholly good. The kinder and more conscientious he is, the more inexorably he will go on

> cutting. If he yielded to your entreaties, if he stopped before the operation was complete, all the pain up to that point would have been useless."[5]

God is like a mother with the tweezers, He doesn't want to cause you pain but He knows that it is for your good to allow for some pain now instead of unending and increasing pain over time. It goes back to the concept of God being on the front lines of the battle, He takes the brunt of the battle as He marches before us, but that doesn't mean we won't face combat. The question becomes: a little combat or a lot? Some pain today or infinitely more pain a month from now? God knows what is for our good.

Imagine if you were in surgery and you woke up mid-surgery from the pain and cried out for the surgeon to stop. At that point the surgeon would have two options: knock you back out (with medicine, of course) and finish the surgery, or stop, leave you open on the table and walk away. Even crying out in your pain, which option would you really prefer? I am no surgeon, so I would really rather not be left lying open on the table still in pain with no knowledge of how to sew myself back up. Similarly, I am not God and I would rather not be left alone with all the pain and suffering that life can throw at me. Keep operating, thank you very much.

Even in the pain of a surgery beauty can come forth, as can, and often does, healing. If God stopped in the middle of spiritual surgery then the pain and suffering would be all for naught. He would seem to be a cruel and evil God for bringing

---

[5] Lewis, C.S. "A Grief Observed." *The Complete C.S. Lewis Signature Classics*. [San Francisco, Calif.]: HarperSanFrancisco, 2002. 674.

about such pain and then leaving us in the midst of it. That is not a God I would want to worship. Thankfully, our God is not some sadistic surgeon who cuts us open just to leave us there to bleed out. He allows, allows *not* causes, pain to enter into our lives, He allows for the tweezers to dig into our hands so that we can be healed. So it is that we find hope even in the most painful surgeries. As the saying goes, the greater the risk, the greater the reward, right? Then it would follow that the more painful the surgery, the more completely and deeply we will be healed and restored. St. Bernard of Clairvaux said, "The piercing nail has become a key to unlock the door, that I may see the good will of the Lord."[6] The scalpels, the tweezers, the pains of life have become a key that opens the door to healing. Pain can open the door to a room filled with the courage to let go of one monkey bar and move forward to the next. Pain becomes a key that opens the door so that we can see the goodness of the Lord and His ability to create light from darkness, beauty from pain, and life from death. Through that door the words that Pocket Full of Rocks sing become all the more true when the band reminds us that God's voice is louder than all of the voices that whisper that we are unworthy. His voice is the sound of love, and His voice is telling a different story. God's voice of love shatters the darkness and breaks through the lies of Satan tenderly calling us to His wide open arms of love. Pain can too easily allow us to think that we are unworthy of being pain-free, but the voice of the Lord is louder than the whispers of our unworthiness. The voice tells us that we can come out of this pain better, stronger, more alive, and more in

---

[6] Saint Bernard of Clairvaux. *Sermons on the Canticle*. *Vultus Christi*. Web. <http://vultus.stblogs.org/2010/03/saint-bernard-on-the-wounds-of.html>.

love with God than ever before. His voice tells a different story as it pushes through the lies, through the darkness, through the pain, and the spiritual surgeries. He calls to us, not just nicely, not just lovingly, but tenderly, with a father's love and care. He waits with open arms to embrace us before, during, and after all the pains of this life if we let go of the pain and hold on to Him. Hear the sound of love. Hear the sound of His voice telling you a different story. He is calling you, are you ready to let go?

Letting Go

Jesus tells Peter that "whatever you bind on earth shall be bound in heaven; and whatever you loose on earth shall be loosed in heaven."[7] Whatever we bind in this life, whatever we hold on to in this life, we will hold on to in the next life. I don't know about you, but the things I find myself holding on to in this life are not things I want to follow me to heaven. I hold on to hurts, to friends doing wrong to me, to heartbreak, bosses that weren't nice to me, to fights with those I love, and to things family members said to me years ago that never sat well. None of those things are things I want with me in heaven and over time I've had to let them go. Neither C.S. Lewis nor Jesus ever specified *when* we have to let go and forgive others; in time – His time – He leads us to a place where we are able to do so. Sometimes it happens quickly, other times it takes longer to come to a place of forgiveness, but He will call us to that place so that we can love Him more perfectly. The important part is to remain open to being led to the place of forgiveness, because He will lead us there.

---

[7] Matthew 16:19.

Sometimes we let things go so that we can grow. Sometimes we have to let other people, like a child or a sibling, go so that they can grow, spread their wings and learn to fly. Sometimes we let go of broken relationships or friendships so that we can find new ones and be valued for who we are, and for what we have to offer others. Sometimes we have to let go of a job that only brings stress into our lives so that we can find one that gives us meaning and purpose. Sometimes letting go is easy and sometimes it is hard. For me, letting go of high school was fairly easy. By the time graduation rolled around I couldn't wait to get out of there, move on with my life, go to college, and meet new people. By the time I graduated from college I wasn't ready to leave. I decided to graduate a year early, and I'm glad I did, but that didn't make letting go any easier. Both instances of letting go were necessary in my life for me to become who God wants me to be, but one was far easier than the other.

Though I would strongly contend there is nothing good that we can learn from Satan, Saint Irenaeus has a theory that I've loved since I first learned about it in college. Most theologians refer to this theory as the "Fishhook Theory". Irenaeus was a disciple of Polycarp, who was a disciple of Saint John, so it is safe to say that this theory has been around for a while and is rooted deep within Tradition. The theory states that since the beginning of time, ever since the Fall of Adam and Eve, Satan has held every person who has ever died in his hands. However, as we state in the Apostle's Creed, Jesus died and descended into Hell. When Jesus descended Irenaeus theorizes that Satan let go of all of the people and reached out for Jesus, the Son of God, and the ultimate prize for Satan. Remember how Satan wants to capture God's children and make them his own and bring them down to join him in Hell? What greater prize could there be for Satan than the *only* begotten Son of God? None. So Satan lets go of all of God's other children and grabs on to Jesus. However, as we all know, Jesus, after three days, rose from the dead. When Satan opened his hands to admire his prize, and probably gloat all about it, he found that his hands were empty because Jesus had risen from the dead and was soon to ascend to Heaven.

What can we learn from Satan and the Fishhook Theory? Unbeknownst to him, he did one thing right, one thing we should all do: let go of everything and everyone else and cling first and foremost to Jesus. The amazing thing, and the amazing difference between us and Satan, is that we will never find ourselves empty handed. Jesus will always be there when we cling to Him, and He made sure of that when He sent us the Holy Spirit. We hold on to so much in our lives, so much baggage and hurt, and yet we are called to let go of all of that and to let it ascend to the Father in heaven who cares for us. We are called to give it all to Jesus who took it all upon Himself as He carried, and then died upon, the cross, underneath the weight of all that we hold on to. He has already died for our burdens, why keep Him nailed to the cross?

Our pains and our burdens weigh us down for a reason, they are not meant to be carried. They can easily become an anchor tying us down to this world. C.S. Lewis once wrote, "God whispers to us in our pleasures, speaks in our conscience, but shouts in our pains: it is His mega-phone to rouse a deaf world."[3]

---

[8] Edwards, Bruce L. *C.S. Lewis: Life, Works, and Legacy*. Westport, CT: Praeger, 2007.

He is speaking into His mega-phone (as if God's voice weren't loud enough). Are you listening? Are you willing to let go? Or are you too busy focusing on all the pain and the hurt because it is all you know? Perhaps we should step out on a limb, let go of what we know and cling to the hope that we find at the foot of the cross. One of the figures that represent God in the book *The Shack* says, "Will you at least consider this: When all you can see is your pain, perhaps then you lose sight of me?"[9] Let us not lose sight of God. Don't miss the forest for the trees, and don't miss the love of God for the pain and the sufferings in your life. Let them go. Let them ascend to God. Cling instead to Jesus, yesterday, today, and forever.

310.

[9] Young, William P. *The Shack*. Newbury Park, CA: Windblown Media, 2007.

Eve and Mary

Just in case you missed the memo, sin has entered the world. It is a nasty little thing that keeps us from being the person God created us to be, and it leads us to believe that we are unworthy. Sin clutters our souls and leaves them in need of a nice, holy shower. Father Chris Kirchgessner, O.S.B. teaches that we learn nothing from sin, except how to sin more. It is illogical to think that we sin so that we can understand what it is like to suffer. I knew a few people in college who were planning on being youth ministers when they graduated, but they spent many of their college nights out partying and hooking up with random guys. They used to say that they were engaging in those activities so that they could relate to the teens in their youth group someday. What a joke. Saying that you sin so that you can eventually understand someone else's struggles or relate to them better is like saying that you are going to put yourself in the middle of a bonfire so that you can relate to the burning wood, it makes no sense. Sure, I'd love to be able to relate to the saints who were burned at the stake and understand all that they went through in their sufferings for Christ, but that does not mean I'm about to go hop into a bonfire. I want to relate to God's children in their sufferings but that does not mean I'm going to go sin and excuse it all for the sake of relating to others. The only thing we learn from sin is how to add to our sins by sinning more. Sin begets more sin. Sinning only makes it easier for Satan to lock us in coffin after coffin, until hope is lost.

Learn from your sins but don't learn *because of* your sins. Learn from your mistakes but don't make the mistake of sinning because you think that's what all people are supposed to do. God knows better. When I went through my semester of stupid decisions in college, I foolishly thought that going out and drinking was what all people my age did, regardless of the legal drinking age. We were in college after all; isn't that what college kids do? I never tried to make the excuse that I was drinking and partying so I could relate to the teens God would someday bring to my youth groups. However, I did try to pass my sins off as something everyone did. Do you know what I learned in all of it? I learned that sin only leads to more sin. Coffin One leads to Coffin Two, and so and so forth. Yes, God has given me opportunities to relate to people in my ministries through my experiences in college. God, in His infinite goodness, can turn something bad (my semester of stupid decisions) into something good: relating to the hearts of His children. But if I could go back, I want to believe I wouldn't make those mistakes again. I never once thought, "Oh, I'll screw up a little here and God will make light of it, so what's the harm?" Not a chance. God is no idiot and justifying my sins in that way would have only served to offend Him, not glorify Him.

Oh, Eve

I would be willing to bet that if you asked Eve if she could change anything in her life, she would take back her decision to eat from the tree of knowledge. True, God has made light even of her sin, as Saint Thomas Aquinas wrote, "O happy fault...which gained for us so great a redeemer!"[1] Even after the Fall I can almost guarantee that Eve wanted to rid her life of sin. Isn't that what we all want? To rid our lives of sin and to live in perfect

---

[1] As quoted in CCC412.

harmony with God and those around us? Of course it is! It is the very thing we were made for, the very state of being for which our heart longs. Eve couldn't rid the world or her life from sin alone. She needed help, just as we need help.

I've heard a number of analogies over the years that describe the difficulty of ridding our lives of sin. Getting rid of sin is like painting a room when you hate to paint. Getting rid of sin is like quitting smoking cold turkey. Getting rid of sin is like training a dog to not pee on your new couch. The analogies go on and on. For me, getting rid of sin is like rearranging a room. Unlike most people I know, I actually love to rearrange rooms and offices. In college I rearranged my dorm room more times than I can count, and those rooms really weren't that big. I rearrange my room, my apartment, and my office as if it were my job. There is something invigorating about a new arrangement of a room. I like the change of pace and the fresh, new feel rearranging can bring to a room.

While I love rearranging rooms, it is quite a bit of work. I usually think about a new arrangement for a few days before I start moving furniture. When I'm actually using the brain that God gave me, I measure my various pieces of furniture to make sure they will fit where I think they will. Finally, the day comes when I carve out a few hours and plan to rearrange the room. The problem is that things never go as fast as I think they will. I move some of the furniture and then realize that I don't really like it as much as I thought I would. Or I move the pieces and then realize that my dresser is too tall for the spot I had planned for it. The dresser blocks all the pictures I have hanging on the wall, so I have to find a new space for those pictures to hang. Like I said, I don't *always* use the brain God gave me! Sometimes I find that I've forgotten my hammer so I can't hang the pictures because I can't put the nails in the wall without it. Or, I (yet again) have forgotten just how heavy my desk is and my arms get too sore and tired to continue moving everything, so pieces of furniture are left in the middle of the room. Sometimes I run out of time, and my room is left a mess, and my furniture is all out of place. The project is far more involved than I originally thought it would be, no matter how much forethought I put into it.

So it is with sin. It would be so much easier if I had someone helping me rearrange my room. Perhaps they could lend me their hammer so I could hang my pictures up somewhere else (they could even spackle the old holes for me!). If I had help then maybe my arms wouldn't get so tired and we could finish the project in one fell swoop. The moving time wouldn't take so long and I wouldn't have to leave the project halfway through it. All the forethought would actually be useful, especially if I had someone helping me. It would be so much easier to rid my life of sin if I had someone to help keep me accountable. I might even be done with sin forever if I had a friend who could bring tools and resources to help me: their Bible, their favorite inspirational book, and the ability to pray for, over, and with me. If I had help getting rid of sin then the project (God willing) would take less time because the work would be divided. If I had help then perhaps I wouldn't get so tired because I would have a cheerleader through it all. Getting rid of sin is like rearranging a room: a great idea that you hope will bring fresh, new life to your soul, but often requires far more work than we think, especially if we do it alone.

Fortunately, we don't have to do it alone. In fact, it isn't even suggested that we do it alone. We were made out of the relationship and community of the Trinity. Therefore, we are made *for* relationship and community, and it is in those relationships that we find the strength to rid ourselves of sin. Sometimes we will fall short, sometimes we'll move a piece of furniture and find that it doesn't fit where we thought it would. So we go to the community and ask for their help. Christ is always with us, in the center of our relationships and communities. It is because He is in the center of them that we find strength and encouragement there.

The New Crown of Creation

We might as well call a spade a spade. Eve, Crown of Creation though she was, failed. She fell short of becoming the woman God created her to be, and we have been falling short ever since. She tried to rearrange her room, so to speak, and found the task at hand to be far more difficult than she had originally anticipated. She fell prey to more than one sin, and each of those sins, each of those downfalls, affects our lives as women today.

Pride is often the first and only sin that people think that Eve committed. Pride comes before the Fall, remember? Pride had Eve thinking that she could be as good and as knowledgeable as God. It told her that God, in some way, no matter how small, was holding out on her. He wasn't giving her everything He had to offer her. Scripture scholars have taught that pride led Eve to think that she *deserved* everything because she was created in God's image. After all, He has it all, why shouldn't she?[2] Pride may have been the first sin that Eve committed, but it certainly wasn't the last one.

By ushering pride in, Eve also became idolatrous. Father Chris Kirchgessner, O.S.B., teaches that in some way, shape, or form all sin is idolatry since all sin is us putting something – money, power, popularity, pleasure, etc. – above our love for God, and our desire to serve and please Him. Eve was idolatrous when she put her own desire for knowledge above her desire to serve and please God. She knew full well that only one tree was forbidden, and that God, being the loving God that He is, had forbidden her and Adam to eat from it. Still, Eve freely chose to eat of the forbidden tree. She chose her own pride and her own selfish desires over her desire to please and love God. She wanted what she wanted and she was going to do what she wanted regardless of the words and commands set down by the Lord Himself. Eve let pride into her heart, and pride brought idolatry along to play, and they continue to hang around to this day. Eve fell short.

Saint Paul describes Jesus as the new Adam, but before there could be a new Adam there had to be a new Eve, a new Crown of Creation.[3] Enter Mary. Eve, in the end, is remembered for her sin, the first sin that ever entered the world. So it follows that Mary, as the new Eve, would be without sin. She is one of only two people throughout history who never sinned, nor was touched by original sin. The other, as we know, is her Son. Mary has appeared and told us, "I am the Immaculate Conception."[4]

---

[2] cf. Eldredge, John & Stasi. *Captivating*. Nashville, TN: Thomas Nelson, 2005. 46-48.

[3] 1 Corinthians 15:45-49; Romans 5: 12-21.

[4] Deery, Joseph. *Our Lady of Lourdes*. Dublin. 1958.

Mary was conceived without sin, and remains untouched by original sin. Eve, too, was created without sin. However sin entered her life and it cast a long, dark shadow over her and her legacy. Through Adam and Eve, God brought about all of humanity. Through Mary and the Holy Spirit, God brought about a new creation, a new humanity. Through Mary, God made the way for a new people, "a chosen race, a royal priesthood, a holy nation, a people of his own."[5]

Mary, however amazing she is, can't be the new Eve, the Crown of the New Creation, simply because she was sinless. Mary is the new Eve because she triumphed in all the ways that Eve failed. Eve was proud, Mary was not. When the angel Gabriel appeared to her to tell her that she would bear the Son of God, Mary didn't respond by saying, *well, it's about time. Of course I will, who else is as awesome as I am?* She didn't respond in pride, but responded in humility. Pride says, *I deserve* while humility says, *I am worthy, not by my own merits, but by the grace of God.* Mary responded to the angel saying, "How can this be?"[6] She wasn't questioning the Lord; rather, she was humbled by what the angel was telling her. In essence she was asking, *who am I, lowly servant girl that I am, to bear the Son of God?* The questioning nature of Mary's inquiry is echoed when she travels to visit her cousin Elizabeth who greets her and asks, "And how does this happen to me, that the mother of my Lord should come to me?"[7] Mary was never proud; she was humble.

---

[5] 1 Peter 2:9.

[6] Luke 1:34.

[7] Luke 1:43.

Also unlike Eve, Mary was never idolatrous. Mary never put her own desires or her own wishes above her desire to serve the Lord. Mary probably never woke up and thought to herself, "I'd love to conceive a child by the Holy Spirit and have no one believe me. That sounds like fun." She may never have dreamt of all that God would ask of her, and she may never have believed she had the strength to follow Him so steadfastly, but she accepted every single thing that God placed before her. Mary responded to the angel saying, "Behold, I am the handmaid of the Lord. May it be done to me according to your word."[8] Mary always chose the will and the commands of the Lord over her own desires or dreams for her life. Mary was completely selfless. She was betrothed to Joseph when the angel Gabriel appeared to her, and according to Jewish laws regarding betrothals, she was to consider him her husband in all things, except for that which leads to children. The risks were high, yet Mary followed and trusted God. Mary shows us the perfect example of what Pope Benedict XVI refers to when he writes, "The only real gift man should give to God is himself. As his religious awareness becomes more highly developed, so his awareness that any gift but himself is too little, in fact absurd, becomes more intense."[9] Indeed, the only gift we should give to God is our whole selves, not just part of us. Mary, as the new Eve, understood this truth and lived it out better than anyone, except for Jesus, who lived His whole life for His Father, just as His Mother did. Mary knew, in her sinless and immaculate heart, that any gift that was less than her whole self was absurd. She gave

---

[8] Luke 1:38.

[9] Ratzinger, Joseph Cardinal. *The Spirit of the Liturgy*. San Francisco, CA: Ignatius, 2000. 35.

everything to God. Mary remained untouched by sin throughout her earthly life, and she is now esteemed as the new Eve, the new Crown of Creation, and is exalted as the Queen of Heaven.

The Ark of the New Covenant

Mary isn't only the new Eve, the new Crown of Creation, and the Queen of Heaven. There are litanies that list many, many names for Mary. She is the Mystical Rose, the Seat of Wisdom, the Mirror of Justice, the Gate of Heaven, the Morning Star, the Help of Christians, the Cause of our Joy, the lists go on.[10] Mary is also the Ark of the New Covenant.[11] In order to understand what it means to exalt and honor Mary as the Ark of the New Covenant, we must first understand what the old Ark of the Covenant was, and why it was so important.

More often than not when most people hear the Ark of the Covenant they tend to think of *Indiana Jones and the Raiders of the Lost Ark*. While that movie points in the right direction, it doesn't do much to explain exactly how fantastic the Ark of the Covenant actually was. In the book of Exodus, God instructs Moses to build an ark. In the plan for the ark, God tells Moses that the ark is to be plated "inside and outside with pure gold, and put a molding of gold around the top of it."[12] Everything about the ark, including the rods that hold the ark up, the rings on the sides of the ark, all of it is to be plated with gold. The ark that Moses was making was perhaps the most magnificent ark that had ever been made. This ark was no ordinary ark, not some run of the mill ark.

---

[10] Litany of Loreto.
[11] Ibid.
[12] Exodus 25:10-22.

God told Moses, "In the ark you are to put the commandments which I will give you."[13] This was the Ark of *the* Covenant, not just any covenant but *the* Covenant. This would be the ark that would hold the Ten Commandments, the Law as given from God Himself to Moses. This was where the word of the Lord would dwell. He would dwell richly within this ark, well plated with gold and highly revered.

In *Indiana Jones and the Raiders of the Lost Ark*, there is a great scene at the end of the movie in which the Ark is opened. In that scene the power within the Ark is so fantastic, so amazing, that Indiana Jones and Marion Ravenwood have to close their eyes so that they won't be killed. Scripture tells us that the Lord told Moses, "no one can see me and live."[14] As Indy and Marion keep their eyes shut, destruction overwhelms the scene around them. People fall and are burned alive. Countless Nazi soldiers meet their death. Fire envelopes nearly everything and a wind bellows all around which only serves to keep the fire growing. Finally, with all of the soldiers and everyone except Indy and Marion dead, all seems to be drawn back into the Ark. The fire fades and what appears to be a great dust tornado ascends heavenward. The lid of the Ark glides on the top of the tornado as it climbs higher and higher into the sky. The clouds open up as the tornado continues to ascend, until all at once the clouds begin to close and the tornado begins to disappear, bringing the lid of the Ark back down to earth. The lid perfectly lands on the Ark, sealing itself shut. Finally, in the silent wake of the aftermath, Indy and

---

[13] Exodus 25: 16.

[14] Exodus 33:20.

Marion open their eyes to see nothing but the golden Ark shimmering in the moon light.

Scripture also tells of the great powers of the Ark. The book of Joshua tells stories of the Ark being carried by priests and separating rivers to open pathways for God's people to walk through.[15] Later, the city of Jericho was overtaken with no more than shouts after the town had been encircled by the Ark.[16] The power of the God that resided in the Ark was simply astonishing.[17] The Ark of the Covenant represented God to His people. It held His words and it held His power. Whenever the Ark was carried it was always wrapped in a veil, in a blue cloth, and was very carefully concealed, even from the priests who carried it. The Ark, which started out as mere wood, was covered in golf and turned into something beautiful and radiant as it housed God Himself.

Do you see how Mary can be seen as the Ark of the New Covenant? Mary came from simple beginnings, from the town of Nazareth. Yet, over time, her true glory was revealed. She housed the Word Made Flesh. She held in her womb the Son of God. As John says at the beginning of his gospel account, "In the beginning was the Word, and the Word was with God, and the Word was God."[18] The Word was God, and He dwelt in Mary. John goes on to say that, "the Word became flesh and made his dwelling among us, and we saw his glory, the glory of the Father's only Son, full of grace and truth."[19] Before Jesus could make His

---

[15] Joshua 4:15-18.

[16] Joshua 6:1-20.

[17] The current location of the original Ark of the Covenant is unknown.

[18] John 1:1.

dwelling among us, He made is dwelling in Mary, the Ark of the New Covenant. Jesus, as the Word Made Flesh, is the New Covenant, and He tells His disciples this at the Last Supper: "This cup is the new covenant in my blood, which will be shed for you."[20] If Jesus is the new covenant, then it follows that Mary is the Ark of the New Covenant. Mary's power, which comes from humility, is so fantastic, so majestic that Satan fears her more than nearly anyone else. Why do you think that in the book of Revelations Satan is trying to "devour her child when she gave birth"?[21] If Satan can destroy the Ark of the New Covenant then he will also destroy the New Covenant Himself, Jesus. The only person Satan fears more than Mary is Jesus. Satan fears Mary because she is the mother of Jesus, Satan's most feared human.

Mary, especially when seen and understood as the Ark of the New Covenant, gives us tremendous hope. The old covenant has not gone away; we have a new covenant and new hope. In a way, the new covenant is like when a couple renews their marriage vows. The old vows have not gone away, but are being reaffirmed in a new marriage ceremony. God has not abandoned us. Mary, as the perfect example of womanhood and of what it means to fully serve God, shines hope in our lives. We have not been born without being touched by original sin and we may not live a sinless life (wouldn't that be nice?), but we have before us an example of a woman who got it right and was richly rewarded for it. Mary is, after all, revered as the Queen of Heaven. Mary

---

[19] John 1:14.

[20] Luke 22:20.

[21] Revelation 12:4.

never stopped striving to serve God. Mary, in all of her radiant goodness, paved the way for Jesus. She made the way for Jesus to live His life recklessly following God, just as she did. Mary never stopped saying yes to God and no to everything that kept her from Him. Where Eve failed, Mary triumphed, and with each triumph we find renewed hope that all is not lost and that we can still be found worthy in God's eyes.

Unwavering Yes

Mary's yes to God was unwavering. She said yes to a sinless life, and she said yes to everything God asked of her, even when it sounded outlandish, foolish or downright insane. She loved God more than she loved herself, so she unfailingly gave her heart, mind, strength, everything to God. Mary could have said no, she had free will. Mary could have said yes once, and then been done, but she kept saying yes, over and over, time and time again. Had Mary said no even once then our salvation history would be radically different. She could have said no to the angel Gabriel when he appeared to tell her about her pregnancy. She could have said she wasn't going to go to Bethlehem with Joseph and perhaps Jesus would have been born in a home and not a barn. As it stands, it was prophetic that Jesus was born in a barn and that His cradle was actually a feeding trough. This symbolizes how He would one day become food for all, even from His lowly beginnings.

Mary could have said no when Joseph woke her so that they could flee to Egypt. She could have left Jesus in the temple when He was twelve and said she was tired of raising Him. She could have said no at the wedding at Cana and Jesus' first miracle may never have happened at such a joyous occasion. She could have said no, she wasn't going to let Him go back to Jerusalem where He would be hung on a cross. She could have walked away as He walked the long road to Calvary, but she didn't. She said yes, every single time, no matter how much it may have pained her heart. Mary's yes, her unwavering, unfailing, unshakable yes made it possible for Jesus to say yes. Mary's example may have been the inspiration Jesus needed to say yes as He prayed to His Father in the Garden of Gethsemane. He prayed for the cup to pass from Him but Jesus, much like His earthly mother, said yes to the will of the Father. At the presentation in the temple Simeon tells Mary "that a sword of sorrow will pierce her heart. Mary does not recoil. Her yes remains pure and uncompromised. Her joy is still complete!"[22] Eve said no, Mary said yes. Eve's decision led to sin, Mary's led to freedom. Mary's yes was pure and changed history and our faith as we know it. What can your yes to God, unfettered, uninhibited, and unconditional do to change history and faith as we know it?

---

[22] "The Presentation." *The Magnificat Rosary Companion*. Chicago: GIA, 1986. 13.

Seen, Sought, Pursued, Worthy

Wouldn't it be wonderful if we could have *started* with this chapter? Starting here wouldn't have done justice to the story. True, we began in perfection, but we aren't there anymore. As sad as that is to admit, we need to assess where we are now so that we can to get back to perfection. We have to come to an understanding of how we got to be the way we are today: broken, flawed, hurting, and lost people. Only in admitting that we are lost can we begin to find our way again. Perhaps, in some weird way, by being kicked out of Eden we are able to see how wonderful it once was, and seeing that paradise lost, as John Milton put it, we will come to hunger and work for it once again. This time, we shall hunger and yearn and work for it, no matter the cost because we know, in the depths of our souls, that it will be worth it. We didn't start at this chapter. So what? So we started as broken people. Our past, our scars, and our brokenness remind us of where we have been; they don't have to direct where we are going, or where we are going to end up.

Despite what the popular t-shirts of a few years ago may have said, Jesus is not, in fact, my homeboy. That phrase never really made sense to me. Jesus, at least for me, is so much more than a "homeboy". Such an understanding of Jesus may have worked for some people. It may have even brought the idea or person of Jesus to a new crowd or scene. If by Jesus being my homeboy you mean that He is my best friend who I love to hang out with and spend time with, then yes, I suppose you could say that Jesus is my homeboy. Jesus, in His infinite glory is more than just my homeboy though; He is my savior, my best friend, my confidant, and most importantly my lover, the first and truest love of my heart. I imagine that, just as thinking of Jesus as my homeboy doesn't always sit well in my mind, some will struggle with the idea of Jesus as lover. But the truth is that He is the kindest, most compassionate lover that anyone could ever imagine. Jesus loves me not only for who I am (as if that weren't enough), He loves my soul, no matter what I've done or where I've been. His love for me is unending, unfailing, and unconditional.

Seen

"Who is there like you, the God who removes guilt and pardons sin for the remnant of his inheritance; who does not persist in anger forever, but rather delights in clemency, and will again have compassion on us, treading underfoot our guilt? You will cast into the depths of the sea all our sins." – Micah 7:18-19

There are so many times I open my Bible, or I take a drive for a beautiful sunset, or the perfect song comes on the radio at the perfect time and I can't help but wonder how anyone could think that God doesn't love them. I read words that the Lord inspired the prophets, like Micah, to proclaim, and I know in the depths of my heart that He is pouring out His love on each one of His children.

As women we struggle to be seen, to feel as though people, and specifically men, see us and truly appreciate our beauty. What we fail to recognize is that God, Jesus (who is fully Man as well as fully divine), and the Holy Spirit love us and have never once taken their eyes or their minds off of us. If God stopped thinking passionately and lovingly about you for even a nanosecond, you would cease to exist. Think about that. Read that verse again from Micah and take in all the love that those words contain. Jesus, the *only* begotten Son of God, sees *you*. He sees you even in your guilt, in your sin, and in your shame and He does not persist in anger forever. Rather He delights in clemency, in mercy, in forgiveness, and in love. He has compassion for us, again and again. He casts into the depths of the sea, and beyond them, our sins. Dear sisters, we are seen by the Most High, and even when we don't want to be seen we are seen, and loved unconditionally and unreservedly.

Sometimes all it takes is for someone to believe in us, to see our beautiful, flawed, confused, majestic feminine hearts and pause to take notice. Sometimes, as the old country song goes, we look for love in all the wrong places and in all the wrong faces and it leads us to the first of many coffins. Even if we have been led to those coffins before it doesn't mean that we can't overcome them and find love in the right face: the face of God. Sanctus Real, in their song, "The Face of Love" sings that God's face is everywhere, from stained glass and colored lights to countless portrayals. In the end the band realizes that we see God better with our hearts than we do with our eyes, noting that God looks more like love every day. We overcome the coffins by seeing Him with our hearts because God is the face of love. John Eldredge, author of *Wild at Heart*, writes,

> "Clairvaux describes Christian maturity as the stage where "we love ourselves for God's sake," meaning that because he considers our hearts the treasures of the kingdom, we do too. We care for ourselves in the same way a woman who knows she is deeply loved cares for herself, while a

woman who has been tossed aside tends to 'let herself go,' as the saying goes. God's friends care for their hearts because they matter to *him*."[1]

The healing of our brokenness and the breaking free from the coffins begins when we stop believing the lies and buying into the garbage that Satan attempts to sell us. The healing continues, and is amplified all the more, when we begin to accept the reality that there is someone who sees us. Deeper still, there is someone who not only sees us, but has never stopped seeing us. Then, by His grace, we begin to look for love in the right places: within His house and His arms, and in the right faces: the face of His Son, especially as He hung on the cross, dying for us. Saint Paul parallels Christ with the Church as His bride when he writes to the church in Ephesus, "For the husband is head of the wife just as Christ is head of the church, he himself the savior of the body."[2] Paul is saying that Christ is the head of the Church who is likened to a wife. Paul goes on to write, "Husbands, love your wives, even as Christ loved the church and handed himself over for her to sanctify her, cleansing her."[3] We look for love in the right places, in the face of Jesus who handed Himself over for us, His bride. Despite the lies that Satan tries to convince us of, and oh, how he tries, we should remember that we are seen, we have always been seen, and we will always be seen by the God who created us in His image. Just as one coffin can all too easily lead to another, so too can believing one truth about the God who loves

---

[1] Eldredge, John. *Waking the Dead*. Nashville, TN: Thomas Nelson, 2003. 213.

[2] Ephesians 5:23.

[3] Ephesians 5:25-26.

us lead to believing another truth until, eventually, we find that we are seen and we are healed.

Sought

"Ever since the days of Adam, man has been hiding from God and saying 'God is hard to find'" – Venerable Archbishop Fulton J. Sheen

The heart of a woman, many people – including women – believe is the most complex thing on the earth. We want chocolate, we want flowers, we want to be left alone…no, wait, we want you to stay. We want men to love us, we want to be wanted, we want men to find us alluring, attractive, sexy, endearing, strong, and passionate, we don't want to be taken advantage of, we want to be appreciated, we want, we want, and we want. We want to be sought after. God not only has His eyes on me, but He looks for me, He watches out for me, He watches over me, and He keeps me safe when I am most afraid. When I say that God seeks us out I mean that He searches for us, He discovers us, and He goes on a quest for our hearts, where ever they may be. I have experienced His search for my heart many times in my life. He comes after us with a love like only He knows, He comes and He saves the day.

There was one night in particular that, even though I refused to admit it then, I knew that God was seeking me out and searching for me. My heart was lost. My heart wasn't just misplaced, it was all-out lost. I was in the middle of that time in college when I made a lot of really bad decisions, but this night in particular was among, if not *the* worst of them all. I had sort of been dating this guy off and on, when we weren't fighting or disagreeing about one thing or another (usually religion or lack thereof). One night, we each had a few drinks at separate parties on campus. We met up at the end of the night and made our way back to his dorm room. We started making out and one thing led to another, and my naïve and not-entirely-sober brain was unsure of exactly what was happening. Before I knew it, clothes were coming off, and I began to cry. He began to laugh at me for crying. Deep down my heart was terrified of what was happening, and what might come next, and his laughter at my pain only served to magnify my ever-growing fear. I was afraid that I didn't have enough control or strength, physically or emotionally, to stop what might happen next. Most of the fine details of that night are a blur, not because of the alcohol (a situation like that will straighten and sober you up pretty quickly), but because I believe God has allowed me to forget. What I do remember is painful, and I remember just enough to know that it would have been all too easy for that night to have ended very differently and for my dignity and self-worth to have been forcefully taken from me. I can honestly say that I've never been more scared in my entire life. I know that if either one of us would have had another drink, or if my heart had been a tiny bit more lost, that night could have ended completely differently than it did. I don't remember how, but I know that I left that room that night with my dignity still intact. I was still ashamed of what had happened, and yet deep down I was so grateful that it didn't go any further. I left that room horrified. I had nightmares and would wake up either screaming or crying, or sometimes both. It took me many nights after that to sleep, for fear of reliving it all in my nightmares, night after night.

That night may have been the scariest night of my life, but it is also a night I can always look back on and know that God loves me, sees me, and searches for my heart. The decision to drink that night was mine, as was the decision to follow that guy back to his room. I can't help but look back on that night now and know that Jesus, my first and truest love, was searching for me, even though my heart was so lost, and even though He was the last person I wanted to give it to, even if I had any idea where it was. That is a night I wouldn't wish on my worst enemy, but if that was what it took to get it through my thick head that God loves me, and He does see me and search for me, then I'd live it again, because the truth and the power of knowing the love that God has for me is far greater than the fear and horror of that night.

Archbishop Fulton Sheen has it exactly right: ever since the time of Adam, we have been hiding from God and then saying that He is the one that is hard to find. In some way, it is kind of like playing hide-and-seek. It is like we are the person who is supposed to be hiding and yet we complain that we can't find the person who is supposed to be finding us. There are roles in the game for a reason. God seeks us, but we also should seek Him. We can't hide from God and then complain that we can't find Him if we are actively hiding ourselves. It makes no sense, and in the end, it only hurts us. I, in my poor-decision-making days, was hiding from God and often complained that He was hard to find. Unfortunately it took a terrifying situation to get it through my stubborn head that He really isn't hard to find. He is always there, all around me, if only I would open my eyes to see Him and be healed and loved by Him.

Pursued

"Get into the habit of saying, 'Speak, Lord' and life will become a romance." – Oswald Chambers

It took a long time for me to realize that not only does God see and search for me, but He also pursues me. The coffins aren't always easy to break out of. In fact, they are rarely easy to break out of. It is no wonder, then, that the journey to recovering and restoring our hearts for His sake is a long one. Realizing His love for us is a difficult task in and of itself; letting God wash you in His all-encompassing love can be even more challenging. I could easily write an entire book about the countless ways that God pursues my heart and yours in just a single day, and I am confident that I would still miss a whole host of ways He does. He pursues our hearts so fervently because His love for us is so intense, and yet we often miss His little gifts of love to us. If you have ever been in a relationship, isn't it the little things that assure you of the love you have for each other? The sweet text in the middle of the day, the note he leaves on your car for you when you get off work, things like that which make our feminine hearts sing? It is the same with God. He sends us little gifts of His love to let us know that He is still pursuing us.

God's pursuit of our hearts looks different for each and every one of us. When we learn, as Oswald Chambers wrote, to say, "Speak, Lord," our life will become filled to the brim with romance because our eyes will be open to seeing the love He pours out on each of us. For some women, God pursues their hearts through music, others through theatre or performing. Still others feel pursued and romanced by God in a chance sighting of a dolphin or the smile of their child. God's pursuit of your heart can't be put into a box because His love for you and His romancing of your heart is specific to you and you alone. He loves you so much that He sends a rainbow in the sky or a thunderstorm to your world at just the right time, just so you know that He loves *you* passionately and deeply.

    I feel God's pursuing love in nature. I see so much of Him in His created world and He wins my heart by revealing His beauty through His creation. My grandmother, at least for as long as I can remember, has always had an exploring and adventurous spirit. She will see a picture of a barn in a magazine, figure out where that barn is and take a trip to see it, simply because she can. People may think she is crazy for taking such trips by herself and exploring the world around us, but it is something I've always admired about her. I love to pick a place on the map and just drive to it. There are beautiful sunny days, and rainy days as well, when I get in my car and have no idea where I want to go. All I know is that I want to hike or drive or see something that takes my breath away. I get on the road and drive until I feel like stopping. I almost never look up trails or maps before I head out. I just go and let the Holy Spirit be my guide. Do you know what happens? I fall in love. Every single time I manage to find some new trail or something stunningly beautiful, and I fall in love with the God who dreamed up such amazing scenery. I find trails with lakes, rivers, wildlife, flowers, and trees. I find trails with mountain tops, abandoned ruins of a presidential summer home, snow in the middle of July, and sights I couldn't imagine in my wildest dreams. I find beauty and I find God. One of my great-grandmothers used to say that we are closest to God when we are in the mountains, and I think she had it right. I find God in a beautiful beach sunset or a thunderstorm rolling in over the sea at night, but mountains are home to me so it is no surprise that I find God dwelling so richly in them.

On one trip in particular, I felt God pursuing me. It was February and I decided to take a week off work and drive to South Dakota by myself. I had never seen Mount Rushmore and I really wanted to go. So I drove, and as I drove through Wyoming, I fell in love with the peace, and when the wind died down, I fell in love with the quiet. There was and is something simplistically serene about Wyoming. I loved driving through the mountains of South Dakota, down the winding and curvy roads as the trees grew out of the mountain sides. There was beauty and majesty there, even if it was still in the dead of winter. It is in God's creation, untouched by cities and cars, that I find God just as He is. Cities can be beautiful, but nature speaks louder to me because it is there that I find the heart of God, wild, unfettered, majestic, lavish, and yet glorious beyond words. He reigns in nature and the beauty abounds and captures my heart, time and time again.

I drove and ended up at Crazy Horse Monument first. I walked around Crazy Horse and took in the beauty of the monument and then made my way to Mount Rushmore before the sun set. Mount Rushmore was amazing, though after seeing Crazy Horse, the size of it paled in comparison. The real gift of that day came as I was leaving Mount Rushmore. As I made my way back to my car, the sun began to set over the Black Hills. The colors that lit up the sky were unlike any I had ever seen, nor could they be accurately captured by my camera. The immensity of the sunset overwhelmed me so much that I stopped before I ever made it to my car just to stare up at the sky and the wonder of it all. In those moments standing there with no one around me, I felt the love of God wash over me as He painted a radiant sunset just for me. He kept me warm despite the winter's chill in the air, and in the stillness I could hear Him whispering to my heart that He loves me and that no matter what happens in this life, He will be there for me and He will always come for my heart.

The next day of that trip was no different. I spent the night in Rapid City, South Dakota and decided to drive to Devil's Tower the next day. One way, the drive would take about two hours and take me back into Wyoming. The drive was beautiful. Before I knew it I could see what I believed to be Devil's Tower in the distance. As I drove closer it grew in size and my heart was ready to burst in anticipation. At long last I made my way to the entrance of the park and as I parked my car I couldn't help but gaze up at the giant tower that stood before me, casting a long shadow with its mightiness. I've never seen any of the movies that featured the tower so I didn't imagine aliens landing there, I just imagined God sitting at the top of that tower.

I decided that I would hike the trail around the tower, even though more than half of it was covered in snow that, at times, went nearly all the way up my legs. It was a beautiful hike and each turn and curve in the somewhat visible path left me even more in awe than the last. The tower itself was beautiful and intimidating, strong and imposing. As I began to reach the side that the sun shined on, and therefore could see the path again, I reached a clearing. I nearly stumbled over my own two feet at the splendor of that sight. I found a bench and began snapping more photos than I can recall, yet they still don't do it justice. I sat there and looked out over a valley that was covered with perfectly white sparkling snow. As I slowly took it all in, I pulled out my journal and thanked God for the wonder of His creation. I thanked Him for romancing me, for pursuing me and my heart, however broken it may be.

    C.S. Lewis writes about the dangers of love and how loving can easily make way for our hearts to be broken. Lewis says that the only place outside of Heaven that we can be safe from all the dangers of love is Hell.[4] In those moments, as I stared out in wonder and awe at that clearing, I realized that there is still beauty in being broken because our brokenness unites us to Christ. There was beauty in that clearing, it may have been cold and nothing may have been growing because it was covered in snow, but even there, in what some may call a desolate place, I found hope and beauty, and I knew that God was romancing my heart.

    I often relive the memories of that trip because they remind me how much God truly loves me and how much He comes for my heart. I know that He continues to pursue me. I know that He continues to pursue your heart. When I think about His pursuit of my heart I recall the words of Saint Augustine, "When I am completely united to You, there will be no more sorrow or trials; entirely full of You, my life will be complete."[5]

---

[4] Lewis, C. S. "Charity." *The Four Loves*. Orlando, FL: Harcourt, 1960. 121
[5] Saint Augustine. As cited in "The Profession of Faith." *CCC* 30.

These little glimpses like the sunset at Mount Rushmore or the clearing at Devil's Tower, are snapshots of what the romance of our hearts is all about: the day when we will finally be united to God.

Worthy

"We change our lives because God's view of love is everything the human heart longs for." – Jason Evert

We have arrived at the section, the reason, and the namesake of this book. This word, this simple truth, is more than a nice title for a book, it is the very reason you and I live and breathe. The truth of this section is that, just as you can lead a horse to water but you can't make it drink, I can lead you to this truth but I can't make you realize it, own it, and make it your own. The knowledge that you are worthy, and, more importantly, that you are worthy in God's eyes, is something you have to come to all on your own. While I may not be able to make you realize this truth, what I can do is walk you to the watering hole and hope and pray that you drink. Here goes nothing.

My parents wanted to name me Ashleigh or Ashley. The name was agreed upon but they couldn't agree on the spelling, so long story short, they ended up naming me Amanda because, thankfully, there is really only one way to spell Amanda. I know that God had his hand in my name because Amanda comes from Latin and literally means "worthy of love" or "worthy to be loved". I've known that about my name for most of my life, but it didn't really have an impact on me until I got older. Who I am, even my very name, reveals the truth I had been looking for over the course of my life. The poor decisions I made in college, the guys I shouldn't have dated, none of them could make me feel as worthy as the name God and my parents gave me. Whenever I begin to doubt that God can overlook my sins or that He can still find me worthy, I think of my name and my fears slowly wash away. In my stubbornness and thick-headedness, I think I needed to be named Amanda to have a constant reminder that no matter who I've become, or how far off the beaten path I've walked, He still finds me worthy, not of just any old love, but of His love, older and more constant than any other.

Even if my name were not Amanda, He would still find me worthy. He hung on the cross out of love for me. He looks at *me* with eyes full, not of judgment, but of love. His body is broken every single day on altars all across the world at Mass. As He is broken in the Eucharist He whispers to each of us, "I am broken for you that you might be whole in Me." What love, what glorious love! Pope Pius XII once remarked that Jesus, whom the world cannot contain, love imprisons in the tabernacle. The world could not and cannot contain the wonder of Jesus, the only begotten Son of God, and yet His love for us imprisons Him in the tabernacle to be continually and perpetually broken for us. He is broken that we may be made whole in Him. The God of the Universe, the Maker of all that is good, is broken for you in an unending message: *you are worthy.*

Jesus doesn't just humble Himself in the Mass and call it good. He remains in the tabernacle, He waits for you and for me in adoration chapels. Even in His vulnerability, He is exposed and open and on display for you as a reminder that you are worthy. In His most humiliated state Jesus was stripped down to nearly nothing, beaten, spat upon, bruised, and hung on a cross to die. Yet through it all, God found Him worthy even when He appeared to be disgusting and worthless to the entire world. Love triumphed. We too are sons and daughters of God, and even when we feel most humiliated, as though we have been stripped down to nearly nothing, beaten and spat upon by the world and left for dead, surely, even then, God finds us worthy.

If and when we find ourselves in such a desolate state and most ashamed, we change our lives, not necessarily because we are tired of living that way, but because we come to discover that God's view of love, and that God, who is Love, is everything the human heart longs for. God is the fulfillment of all our works and desires. God loves us because we are *His*. He finds us worthy of an unending, unchanging, unconditional love. Our names may as well all be Amanda because He finds each and every one of us worthy of His unconditional love.

There is a song sung by Jason Mraz called, "I Won't Give Up". One of my favorite things to do when I listen to music is to imagine God in the lyrics, or to imagine Him singing them to me. Imagine God singing a song to you about how He won't give up on you. In this song He tells you that looking into your eyes is like watching a night sky light up with the stars or the sunrise paint the sky with its beauty. The chorus comes crashing in as He sings that He won't give up on you, no matter how rough the skies get, He will give you **all** of His love. God continues to sing to you telling you that you are worth it, you are worth the wait, and no matter how long He has to wait, He'll be there patiently waiting for you to come home to Him. Unlike so many before Him, God tells you that

He doesn't want to be someone who walks away. In fact, He will never walk away. God is here to stay and to let His love make all the difference in your life. Again and again the chorus rings out, reminding you that God will never, ever give up on you. He knows you are tough, He knows you can be stubborn, but He wants you to know that you are loved, and that you are worth it. Let Him romance you, let Him pursue you. Allow Him to show you how worthy He finds you. Look up. Find the Love that has always found you worthy.

The Proposal That Never Ends

"To fall in love with God is the greatest of all romances; to seek Him, the greatest adventure; to find Him, the greatest human achievement." – St. Augustine

In every epic love story there are three main parts, or acts. Act one begins with a great love: two people meet, they have an amazingly personal relationship, and they fall in love. Act one ends, as we know from countless chick flicks, with separation. Someone leaves, someone gets hurt, someone gets a job offer and moves away, or someone dies. The reasons are as numerous as the stars, but separation occurs. Act two begins in the wake of that separation and brings us through the struggle and the agony, the search for love and peace. The second act is what takes up most of the time in the classic chick flicks; it is the part of the story that is filled to the brim with drama. The separation is what we remember most because it tears at our heart strings. The second act is what all too often breaks our hearts as we connect with the characters and relate to their struggles. Act two is where we think the story ends because it is what we remember, it is what haunts us. What we forget is that act two does end, and it usually ends with at least one sacrifice. Someone gives up a job offer, admits they were too prideful to commit, someone apologizes, or someone sacrifices so that the curtain can close on act two. The third act is the reunion: the lovers reunite in some fantastic scene in the rain, or the snow, or on the top of the Empire State Building. Act three is bursting with peace and freedom and love. The bounds of love have been tested and the lovers have been reunited, their love has overcome act two and the credits begin to roll. Every good love story follows this path. This is how every love story is supposed to end; this happy ending is the ending that is written on our hearts.

We believe we are, for the better part of our lives, in the middle of act two. We started our lives as creations of the Most High, in love with Him in our childhood innocence. We, at some point, fell in love with Him. Then act one ends. We are separated; we realize that we aren't in Eden and that this life is messy and painful. The world, we come to find to out, isn't always nice to us. We find ourselves in a coffin and don't know how to get out, and we are separated from the love of God. The drama fills and consumes our lives and we are left searching and struggling for answers, for happiness, for hope, and for love. We spend most of our days in the midst of this struggle, too stubborn to realize that the sacrifice that ends act two has already taken place. Perhaps you have heard of a man by the name of Jesus. He made the ultimate Sacrifice to end act two of this epic love story once and for all. He made that sacrifice so that you and I could be reunited with Him and His Father. Jesus paid the price so that you could have peace, life to the full, and unending freedom.[1] Blessed Pope John Paul II said, "God passionately desires and ardently yearns for our salvation...nothing is greater than this: that the blood of God was poured out for us."[2] His Sacrifice made the way for act three to begin so that we can live out our days in act three. This

---

[1] John 16:33, John 10:10, John 3:16-21.

[2] Blessed Pope John Paul II. "General Audience - February 18, 2004." *General Audience - February 18, 2004*. Vatican.
<http://www.vatican.va/holy_father/john_paul_ii/audiences/2004/documents/hf_j p-ii_aud_20040218_en.html>.

play, this epic love story, ends in Heaven where the curtains are closed and we are fully reunited with God, and peace and freedom abound. Just because the epic love story ends in Heaven doesn't mean we can't live in act three every day for the rest of our lives.

The Brink of Death

The truth is that ever since sin entered the world we have been on the brink of death and we have remained there, until Christ came to give His life for us. Think of the princess stories you heard growing up and the classic tales you watched unfold countless times as you made your parents play those movies over and over again. What brought Snow White back from the brink of death (after eating a poisoned apple no less)? True love's kiss. What awoke Sleeping Beauty? True love's kiss. In *Enchanted*, when Giselle falls under the evil witch's spell, what awakens her? True love's kiss. What allowed Ariel to get her voice back from Ursula? True love's kiss. True love's kiss brings the princesses back from the brink of death. We too, as daughters of the King of Kings, are princesses. What brings the heart of a woman back from the brink of death, after sin and suffering have entered the world and threaten to overwhelm her life? True love's kiss just won't do. What brings back the heart of a woman is *the* proposal that never ends.

There was a time, years ago, when Jesus walked the Earth, that proposals happened differently than they do now. In those days when a man wanted to propose to a woman, he didn't buy a ring and get down on one knee. He first asked for her father's permission. If he was given permission, he would have a meal or some type of a gathering with her family. At this gathering, he would offer her a cup of wine, usually a red wine. This wine symbolized his life, the very blood that kept him alive. He offered it to her as a sacrifice, and if she accepted his proposal, she would drink of the same cup, she would drink his life into her own. Then she would offer the cup back to him, which now symbolized her life, and he would drink of it as well. The gesture was highly symbolic as both of them had each other's' blood flowing within them. Their lives had become one. After this sharing of the wine, the man would leave and act one was over. The man didn't leave because he disliked the woman; he left because he had to go to his home-town, or wherever his father lived, to build a house for his new bride. The man would build a dwelling attached to his own father's house, where he would bring his bride to, and they would raise their family. During this time the two lovers typically would not see each other. Ordinarily, the man's best friend would act as a go-between, passing messages of love and hope between the couple as the man built the house and the woman waited for the day that she would go with her husband to their home. The woman never knew the day that she would go home with her husband, so she was in a constant state of readiness, eagerly awaiting the day of fulfillment. Act two, in those days, was full of waiting and struggle as the weather, supplies, and the season all dictated how quickly the man could finish building their dwelling. Act two ended when the sacrifice of building the house was complete. The man would run to his beloved and finally take her home to be his bride, his wife, and his best friend for the rest of their days.

That sounds like a love story I always wanted to be a part of until one day it hit me: I am a part of that love story. I am the beloved. We are all the beloved. Doesn't this story sound at all familiar? Jesus asked His Father and our Father for permission to marry you. He loves you so much that He wants to be united to you forever, which is why He came to Earth, humbled Himself by becoming human, and freed you from sin and death. He was sacrificing for you from the beginning, from the time that He humbled Himself to be born of a virgin. God the Father, being the loving and compassion Father that He is, granted Jesus permission to marry you. So Jesus had a feast, the Last Supper. He gathered all of His closest friends and offered them, not just an ordinary cup of wine, but a chalice of wine. A chalice is a fancy, elaborate cup: a sacred vessel, worthy of only the finest and most sacred wines. Jesus offered His friends this chalice as He said, "Take this, *all of you*, and drink from it, for this is the chalice of my blood, the blood of the new and eternal covenant, which will be poured out for you and for many."[3] Jesus was proposing to His apostles, to His friends, and to us. He wanted all of us, His children, to drink from the chalice of His blood so that we would be betrothed to Him. This wine was no longer a symbol; it was and is His blood so that we would literally have His life in our veins. This is the blood of the new and eternal covenant; this is the blood that makes the way for a proposal that never ends. Jesus asked us to do this, to celebrate the Last Supper, in remembrance of Him. The proposal didn't just happen once, it happens literally hundreds of thousands of time across the world every day when Mass is

---

[3] Roman Missal, Eucharistic Prayer I, emphasis added.

celebrated. The proposal happens every time we go to Mass; Jesus is proposing to us again and again. What love could be greater than that, to propose to you every day of the week, and every day of the year? He has been proposing to you, and to all of His children, in every Mass that has been celebrated since the Last Supper. I could think of no more amazing love than to keep proposing to us, time and time again. No matter how many times you have said no before, He keeps proposing, hoping, waiting, and praying that this time, this day, will be the day that you say yes. Will you accept His proposal?

There is more! When we accept His proposal, He takes the cup back and drinks our life into His, and He carries it with Him to the cross. As we know, Jesus left us when He died on the cross. That was how a proposal in those days went. Jesus left to go build us a house attached to His Father's house so that one day He can take us there to be with Him forever. Jesus tells us, "In my Father's house there are many dwelling places. If there were not, would I have told you that I am going to prepare a place for you? And if I go and prepare a place for you, I will come back again and take you to myself, so that where I am you also may be."[4] Jesus tells us this out of love, pure and true love, that even though He is going away, He will come back again and take us to Himself. He doesn't say He might come back, or that if we are lucky He will come back, He says that He *will* come back for us. We do not know the day or the hour He will come, which is why we are called to be awake and alert and constantly ready for Jesus to take us Home with Him.

---

[4] John 14:2-3.

Still, there is more light to be shed on this amazing proposal and the most epic love story ever told. In the days when Jesus was alive, the man typically had a best friend who would relay messages between the lovers as they waited for the dwelling to be finished so that they could finally be reunited. Jesus has such a best friend that He sends to us with messages of love and hope as we eagerly await the day that our beloved will come for His bride. Jesus tells us,

> "If you love me, you will keep my commandments. And I will ask the Father, and he will give you another Advocate, to be with you always, the Spirit of truth, which the world cannot accept, because it neither sees nor knows it. But you know it, because it remains with you, and will be in you. I will not leave you orphans; I will come to you."[5]

Jesus sends us the Holy Spirit, the Advocate to relay those messages of love between us and Jesus as we wait for Him to finish building our dwelling in Heaven. The Spirit of truth will remain with us and will be in us. Jesus again promises us that He will not leave us orphans or abandoned.

The proposal has been laid out before you, and it is on offer every time Mass is celebrated. Jesus comes before you, so in love with you that He offers you His cup, His chalice, His blood, and His life. Will you accept? Will you drink of His chalice?

No Death Do Us Part

Jesus, as we know, not only triumphed over sin, He also triumphed over death. His triumph over death gives us hope that,

---

[5] John 14:15-18.

with His help, we can also triumph over death so that we can live in act three of this story of unending love. We die to the things that keep us from God so that we can live in Him. We die in this life so that we can rise to an eternal life in Heaven with the first and truest love of our lives. When we die, Jesus invites us Home; He comes back for us and brings us to the dwelling that He has prepared for us with His Father so that we can be eternally united with Him.

Act three exists in this life if we allow for it. Jesus came to offer us peace, and He is reunited with us through the Holy Sacrifice of the Mass. As Sanctus Real sings in their song "Eternal", the marriage of our hearts to God's leaves out the "death do us part" because God is eternal, and we are eternally His. When Jesus proposes to us and we say yes, our hearts are united in a bond so strong that not even death can break it. In the Song of Songs, we read some of the most intense and poignant words about the love of God and the depth of His love for us, "Set me as a seal on your heart, as a seal on your arm; for stern as death is love, relentless as the nether world is devotion; its flames are a blazing fire. Deep water cannot quench love, nor flood sweep it away. Were one to offer all he owns to purchase love, he would be roundly mocked."[6] The bond that unites our hearts to Jesus' heart cannot be quenched or washed away; it is as stern as death and set as a seal on both of our hearts. Jesus is eternal and by saying yes to Him, we become eternally His. The proposal never ends in this life. The marriage is made complete in Heaven

---

[6] Song of Songs 8:6-7.

where act three, and the greatest love story ever told, comes to its precipice – the eternal reunion of our hearts with Jesus's.

Sanctus Real goes on to list a myriad of things that could never separate us from God's love. As Saint Paul writes in his letter to the Romans, "I am convinced that neither death nor life, nor angels, nor principalities, nor present things, nor future things, nor powers, nor height, nor depth, nor any other creature will be able to separate us from the love of God in Christ Jesus our Lord."[7] There is absolutely nothing that could separate us from the love of God. We can never lose Him to sickness, or divorce, or life, or death, or anything, ever. With God there is no concept of abandonment. We are safe within His arms because there is no death do us part. There is no anything do us part. Could there be a greater third act than the promise that nothing could ever separate us from the Love of Christ?

Venerable Archbishop Fulton J. Sheen once said, "The greatest love story of all time is contained in a tiny white host." That love story continues in you and me. The love story is not over: we are not all in Heaven, at least not yet. Enjoy the proposal that happens every single day. Drink of the love that never ends. Rest your heart in the knowledge that there is no concept of abandonment, and that we are always safe within His arms. We have everything in Him. Our hearts find the love that we have been searching for all along and we are made whole in His love. There are no coffins here, no lies, and no half-truths. There is only love, truer, deeper, and more faithful than you will find anywhere

---

[7] Romans 8:38.

else. Why are we still looking for love? Why do we search for love, as if God is not enough? The search is over, the Answer is here.

Fragile, Handle With Care

The story sounds fantastic and if we lived in a perfect world, we would all be sold on the beauty and the magnificence of the story alone, but we don't live in a perfect world. Our hearts are fragile and we need to know that they will be handled with care. How can we know that our hearts will be loved and cared for? John Eldredge sums it up well when he writes, "When it comes to the whole subject of loving others, you must know this: how you handle your own heart is how you will handle theirs."[8] How do we know if Jesus will handle our hearts with care? We see how He cared for His own heart. He willingly allowed it to be pierced out of love for you and me. Does that mean He will allow our hearts to be pierced? Not necessarily. His heart was pierced only through and because of His great love. Surely, if our hearts are to be pierced, He will fill them to the brim with love to withstand the pain of being pierced. How do you think His heart was pierced? It first had to be filled with Love. How else did He handle His heart? He constantly trusted it to His Father and always placed it in His care. Rest assured that this is exactly how He will handle our hearts, with an abundant love that will always place our hearts in the loving hands of God the Father.

Love is the answer to the question that is written deep within our feminine hearts, *"Am I worthy?"* God, who is Love, is the answer to that question. Love is always the answer. The

---

[8] Eldredge, John. *Waking the Dead*. Nashville, TN: Thomas Nelson, 2003. 211.

Answer has been here all along, we've just been too locked in our coffins to see the triumph of Love. We've been locked in the dark; we've missed the light and beauty of the Sacrifice that has already taken place and thrust us from act two into act three. What a glorious wonder to wake up and break free from our coffins and find ourselves in the middle of the greatest love story the world has ever known! Life is always better when we are with Jesus. Life is better when we don't try to go it alone and we wake to the awe-inspiring truth that we are loved and we are worthy, beyond even our wildest dreams. Tyrone Wells sings of this truth in his song, "This Love". In it, Wells describes a love that desires to pour itself over you and washes you clean. The love that Wells sings of may as well be God's love crying out to each of us, telling us that we are beautiful just as we are, and that we no longer have to hide our scars. If we but come to God, He will help us learn to see that we are beautiful just as we are, all we need to do is go to God. Going to God, we will see how desperately and longing He wants to pull us close to Him until we know and feel and live and breathe His love. God invites us to listen to the rhythm of His heartbeat and know that with every drop of blood, His love is echoing.

God sees that you are beautiful *just as you are.* He doesn't want you to hide your scars, He wants to heal them. He desperately wants to pull you close and be healed by His love. With every drop of blood that He poured out on the cross His love is echoing, telling us that all we need is Him. Draw yourself close to Him until you know and feel and live and breathe His love.

If you find yourself in the middle of act two of this epic story, remember that we were not made for act two; we are made for act three. We were made for Heaven, for love, happiness, joy, hope, peace, and worthiness. Jesus came so that we could be free to live all our days in the middle of act three, in the midst of the most epic romance, and most fantastic and magical love story ever told. Return your heart to Him. He is waiting for you. He longs to propose to you, again and again, so that you would never forget or doubt the depth of His love for you. Your beloved yearns to be united with you. Open your heart to the romance and the love He has for you. He is bursting at the seams to shower you and overwhelm you with His eternal love. Remember the words of Saint Augustine, "To fall in love with God is the greatest of all romances; to seek Him, the greatest adventure; to find Him, the greatest human achievement." Fall in love with Him. Seek Him. Find Him. He is waiting for you.

The Truth and the Challenge

"Facts do not cease to exist because they are ignored." – Aldous Huxley

"Life is a daring adventure or nothing at all." – Helen Keller

Invitation

Welcome to the truth. You are worthy, and you are worthy of a love beyond your wildest dreams. Still, somehow, we find it all too easy to forget, doubt and question this simple truth. We may forget, but God never does. He always seeks to remind us of His love for us. So why do we forget? Because the world screams lies at us and tries to lead us, and sometimes shove us, back into those coffins we have finally escaped from. We, by the love of Christ, have broken free of the darkness of those coffins. We have been exposed to the Light and we aren't about to forsake it anytime soon. Re-read the first section if you must, but don't forget that the Father of Lies repeatedly whispers half-truths and lies to us: we aren't seen, we aren't noticed, we aren't sought after, we aren't being pursued, and most of all, we are not worthy of love or any good thing that life has to offer us. Sometimes the un-truths come in whispers, nearly indistinguishable from our own thoughts. Sometimes they come in screams. At times the lies are easy to recognize, but all too often they come in so slowly that we believe they are our own doubts, not the work of Satan. The doubts, the insecurities, and our own imperfections are always before us and threaten to bury us alive. The doubt builds and the lies become entrenched in our hearts and souls until we find that, once again, we are handing the hammer and nails over to Satan, asking him to lock us away again. The lies become a part of who we are, unless we choose to believe that someone somewhere wants more for us.

Forgotten Reality

We, as children of the Most High, were made for more. We were made, not for original sin, but for original glory. Our original glory is deeper to our nature; it is engrained on our hearts and souls. As Saint Stanislaus Kosta once said, "I want eternity, I was born for greater things." Our original glory is awakened when we encounter the unending love of Christ because He lives in original glory. What defines who we are is not our sin, but rather the glory that we were created in the image of, and the glory for which we were created. This glory is the promise that the psalmist writes of, noting, "In my heart I treasure your promise, that I may not sin against you."[1] We treasure the promise of love, the promise of hope, and the promise of a return to glory in anticipation that we would live as upright people all of our days, as a people set apart for His glory. The tragedy of original sin is that it has led us to believe that authentic, unending, perfect love is no longer possible for us. This is yet another lie that must be exposed because we were made to know, experience, and participate in authentic love.

Saint Augustine wrote, "The single desire that dominated my search for delight was simply to love and to be loved."[2] This is our forgotten reality, the truth that we were made for more than this world, that we were made for more than the doubt and insecurities that plague our lives. Saint Augustine said it best when he said that the single desire that dominates his, and therefore our, search for delight is simple: to love and be loved. If

---

[1] Psalm 119:11.

[2] Saint Augustine. "Book II." Trans. Henry Chadwick. *Confessions*. Oxford: Oxford UP, 1992. 24.

we really believe this truth then we find ourselves constantly searching for love. Don't we already know this to be true? Whether it is from our parents, our peers, the cute guy that just walked by, or the love of God, we are, and have always been, searching for love. Once we have encountered, in however small a way, the love of Christ, something in our hearts is awakened. Something within us sits up and takes notice. When this happens we do one of two things: seek Him out, or try to forget that we were ever touched by so a deep a love.

When we seek Him and we find Him, we are complete in Him. The classic line from *Jerry Maguire*, "You complete me" becomes laughable because we know that the only love on the face of this planet that ever completes us is Christ's. Alternatively, when we try to forget that we were ever touched by so deep a love, we still hunger for love and try to find it in other places. We fear the depth of His love and we fear that if He really and truly knew us, the love He has for us wouldn't be so deep. We fear that His love for us will turn out to be as shallow as the so-called 'loves' we have already encountered. So we go on searching, trying to forget His love and we come up short, or even empty, time and time again. In time we find our way to the comfort that Satan's coffins offer us and the 'protection' they offer our hearts. The choice remains ours once we encounter Him: do we love Him, and submit our lives to Him, and find within His heart the beauty of surrender, or, will we walk away from His embrace and return to the sad but familiar lies that Satan has sold us on? Will we let our guards down and allow ourselves to be loved, truly and completely, or, will we continue to search for love in all of the wrong places?

Pope Benedict XVI once said, "God loves us; we need only summon up the humility to allow ourselves to be loved." It takes humility for love to happen and flourish. We build the walls up around our hearts until we are sure that we won't be hurt again. What we forget as we build up those walls is that, while nothing may ever hurt us behind them, no joy can penetrate there either. It takes humility and courage to lower the walls that we build around our hearts and allow love to enter in. True love requires humility of both parties involved. God already humbled Himself when He came to be born of the Virgin, all that remains is for us to humble ourselves and allow His love to lift us up and change us into the people we were created to be. As Saint Paul wrote in his letter to the Philippians, "Rather, he emptied himself, taking the form of a slave, coming in human likeness; and found human in appearance, he humbled himself, becoming obedient to death, even death on a cross."[3] One being in this relationship has already humbled Himself, the love becomes complete when we humble ourselves and allow Him to enter into our hearts.

The love of God is not something we should fear, nor is it the kind of love that causes us pain. His love brings joy and goodness to our lives. Despite the pains and heartaches of life, His love is greater still. It would be relatively easy to write an entire book about the ways that God loves us; there simply aren't enough adjectives in all of the languages in the world to describe the depth and width and breadth of God's infinite love for us. As

---

[3] Philippians 2:7-8.

George Strait sings in his song "My Infinite Love", God wants us to know that it will be Him and His infinite love for us, just as He has always promised us. God's love will always be there, we need only summon the courage and the humility to allow Him to break our walls down and shower us in His love.

The truth is that, as Albert Einstein said, "There are two ways to live your life: one is as though nothing is a miracle, the other is as if everything is." We can choose to look at the world through the lenses of Satan, and believe you me, they are no rose-colored sunglasses. However, when we look at the world through the eyes of faith, we see everything as a miracle. From the trees growing and blooming in the spring, to the snow falling in the winter, and from the miracle of a child being conceived and born, to watching that child have their own children, everything is a miracle. The simple to the magical, when seen through the eyes of faith, is miraculous. Once again, the choice is ours, but I would much rather see everything as a miracle, as the wondrous love of God poured out on His children.

The Challenge of a Lifetime

How many times do we wish the story would just end? We watch a great romance unfold, and though we know that pain and suffering and challenges will come, we want to end the story, turn off the movie before the pain enters in. We watch a great sports game and our team is winning at half-time and we'd like to just call it a game and walk away winners. We want the story to end when we are happy, and we want it to end before the inevitable pain comes in. The beauty of our story is that pain has already entered in and we, by the grace of God and the proposal that never ends, have overcome it. We have escaped from the coÿins and we have been found worthy by the love of God. But the story is not over. It is not half-time, it is not the middle of the movie. We are playing in overtime now. We are playing for bonus points, extra credit, bragging rights, and all the guts and glory that the universe can offer us. We are being challenged to keep the happy ending going long after the credits have rolled off the screen. But we can't keep the happy ending going alone, we need help, we need each other. Pope Benedict XVI once said, "Let unifying love be your measure, abiding love your challenge, self-giving love your mission."[4] We are being challenged to love and to keep on loving, even in the face of doubt, insecurity, countless lies, and untold pain. We are being challenged to stand up and live as daughters of God who are worthy. We are not called to shrink behind our coffins or our masks of fear and doubt. Rather, we are being challenged to an abiding and unending love that moves us to be more than we already are. We are being challenged to give of ourselves, and to make that love our life's mission. If we are honest with ourselves, this challenge will take us the rest of our lives to complete. We doubt that Love really abides within us, probably more often than we would care to admit should Jesus come knocking on our doors. We question the abiding love that seeks to make His home in our hearts, which is why we need the rest of our lives to complete this challenge, however long that may be.

---

[4] Pope Benedict XVI. "World Youth Day Homily." Speech. World Youth Day. Randwick Racecourse, Sydney, Australia. 19 July 2008. *EWTN*. Eternal Word Television Network. Web.
<http://www.ewtn.com/library/PAPALDOC/b16wyd08vig.htm>.

The wonderful truth about this challenge is that we can't do it alone; we need others to help us in our struggles. We need other women to help us in our times of need, and those times will come. Satan will come knocking with those old doubts and insecurities, of this I am sure. He will try to lead us to believe that even though we may have overcome some of our imperfections, there are infinitely more flaws about us that we have yet to overcome. When Satan does come with old and new insecurities, we lean on the women in our lives who struggle as we struggle, and we find strength in one another. Yes, our male friends can offer us support and encouragement, but the truth of the matter is that they are not hard-wired in the same way that women are. God made the sexes to complement each other, not to clearly and perfectly understand each other. We go together like peanut butter and jelly but no matter how hard they try, peanut butter will never understand what it is like to be jelly, and vice versa. As great as salt and pepper go together, salt can never be or understand pepper, nor can pepper understand or be salt. Salt relates to salt, pepper relates to pepper. So too, we need women in our lives, good female friends who can understand and relate to our own feminine hearts. The same is true of men, they need men in their lives, good male friends who can understand and relate to the struggles that they face as men. Women are relational in a different way than men, and we are invited to be that kind of relationally good friend, confidant, and support to each other. The sexes each bring something special to the table when it comes to dealing with and working through the struggles of this life, but there is something special, something sacred even, to sisterhood and brotherhood, it helps us to be validated in our own struggles, and gives us hope that we are not alone.

The challenge of a lifetime has always been there, though we don't recognize or acknowledge it until we allow God to break down the walls around our hearts. This challenge waits until the veil is torn and we see the Light of the Truth that we are worthy. In ancient Judaism there was a veil that covered the Holy of Holies. The Holy of Holies is the inner sanctuary of the tabernacle in the Jewish Temple. During the First Temple, also referred to as Solomon's Temple, the Ark of the Covenant was kept in the Holy of Holies. Solomon's Temple was eventually destroyed. Even after the destruction of the First Temple, the Holy of Holies was a very sacred place that only the High Priest could enter once a year on the feast of Yom Kippur. This veiled sanctuary was the most sacred place that anyone could enter. This most sacred place was understood to be the true dwelling place of God. However, immediately following Christ's death on the cross the gospel writers tell us, "behold, the veil of the sanctuary was torn in two from top to bottom."[5] The veil was torn by Christ's death so that everyone could enter into the Holy of Holies. Through His death, all people have access to the inner sanctuary because Christ is the inner sanctuary. He tore the veil so that our eyes would be opened to seeing the beauty, the divine, and the miraculous through Christ. The veil had to be torn so that we could all have direct access to God every day of the year, just as the veil has to be torn back from the lies so that we can come to the Truth ourselves. When we come to this truth, to the reality that we are

---

[5] Matthew 27:51, Mark 15:38

made worthy and that, despite our shortcomings, we are still worthy of His love, we are challenged to live differently.

No More Hiding

The cat is out of the bag and the truth has been revealed. We can no longer hide from the fact that we are not only seen, sought, and pursued, but we are also worthy of love, and a divine, unconditional love at that. What happens when truth has been revealed to us? It changes us. Think of Lizzy in *Pride & Prejudice*, once she knows that Mr. Darcy loves her. She is changed by Mr. Darcy's love, even if she finds it repulsive at first. When the apostles hear word that Jesus has been raised and the tomb is empty, the truth changes them and their mission in life. When Jesus reveals His risen self to them, they can no longer hide in the Upper Room "for fear of the Jews," rather, they are moved by the peace that Jesus brings them, to go out into the world and preach about the Son of God.[6] Jesus tells His disciples, "Peace be with you. As the Father has sent me, so I send you."[7] Jesus said that as much to the apostles as He says it to us today. The reality of our worthiness fills us with peace and so we are also sent. Sent where? Out into the world to share the good news, to live as women filled with peace, and who radiate the love of Christ.

Stasi Eldredge writes, "We don't get to stay in hiding until we are whole; Jesus invites us to live as an inviting woman now, and find our healing along the way."[8] The battle is far from over. Just because we know that we are worthy doesn't mean that we

---

[6] John 20:19.

[7] John 20:21.

[8] Eldredge, John & Stasi. *Captivating*. Nashville, TN: Thomas Nelson, 2005. 138.

are invincible, nor does it mean that we are perfectly healed. Just because the apostles knew that Jesus had risen from the grave doesn't mean that they were invincible or perfectly healed either, and yet they were challenged to live as radical missionaries for Christ, and they found healing and purpose along the way. Similarly, we are challenged to live differently in our new reality, we are challenged to come out from hiding and find our healing along the way. We are healed by striving to live as the women that God created us to be, and by falling deeper in love with Him. As Blessed Pope John Paul II said, "we are not the sum of our weaknesses and failures, we are the sum of the Father's love for us and our real capacity to become the image of His Son Jesus."[9] If we believe, and if we cling to our God-given worthiness, then we can become the image of Jesus. After Blessed Mother Teresa received Communion she would pray, "Dear Jesus…flood my soul with Your spirit and life. Penetrate and possess my whole being so utterly, that my life may only be a radiance of Yours…let them look up and see no longer me, but only Jesus!"[10] May this simple prayer be the prayer of our hearts. May we decrease so that He may increase, so that when people look at us they may see the face of God. God assures us through the prophet Jeremiah, "I will restore you to health; of your wounds I will heal you, says the Lord."[11] Be assured that He will heal us of all our wounds and restore us to health of body, mind, and soul. Hide-and-seek is over

---

[9] Pope John Paul II. "Solemn Mass Homily." Speech. 17th World Youth Day. Downsview Park, Toronto. 28 July 2002. *The Vatican*. Web. <http://www.vatican.va/holy_father/john_paul_ii/homilies/2002/documents/hf_jp-ii_hom_20020728_xvii-wyd_en.html>.

[10] Blessed Cardinal John Henry Newman. *The Fragrance Prayer*.

[11] Jeremiah 30:17.

dear sisters, Christ has found us and it is our turn to seek others who don't yet know or believe that we are seen, sought after, pursued, and worthy of love.

The reality of our worthiness is not something that can or should be hidden. The truth that we are worthy is like a light that fills us up and radiates from our inner being. Light, as we know, cannot truly be hidden. Jesus said,

> "No one who lights a lamp hides it away or places it under a bushel basket, but on a lamp stand so that those who enter might see the light…take care, then, that the light in you not become darkness. If your whole body is full of light, and no part of it is in darkness, then it will be as full of light as a lamp illuminating you with its brightness."[12]

We, to whom Love has been revealed, are a light and we are not to be hidden under a bushel basket. When others enter into our lives they should be able to see the light that is within us. We are to be put on a lamp stand and allow Him to take care of us, so that we remain in the light of Truth. Filled with His love we can be illuminated and share the light of His love with others. As Saint Augustine said, "let the root of love be within, of this root can nothing spring but what is good."[13]

If we are honest with ourselves, what do we really fear? Do we fear being inadequate? Certainly. Do we fear greatness? Perhaps. What is our greatest fear? As Marianne Williamson puts it,

---

[12] Luke 11:33, 35-36.

[13] Saint Augustine. "Homily 7 on the First Epistle of John." Speech. *New Advent*. Web. <http://www.newadvent.org/fathers/170207.htm>.

> "Our deepest fear is not that we are inadequate. Our deepest fear is that we are powerful beyond measure. It is our light, not our darkness that most frightens us...You are a child of God. Your playing small does not serve the world...we are all meant to shine...we were born to make manifest the glory of God that is within us. It's not just in some of us; it's in everyone. And as we let our own light shine, we unconsciously give other people permission to do the same."[14]

Our playing small does not serve the world, nor does it please or bring glory to God. It is time to let our light shine; it is time to make manifest the glory of God that is within each of us. It is time to let our worthiness shine so that others may not only realize their own light, but let it shine as well.

It doesn't end here. Our story doesn't end with the amazing revelation and life-changing truth that we are worthy. We are challenged to live as inviting women now, challenged to find healing along the way, challenged to let our light shine and not hide it under a bushel basket, or in the darkness of coffins. How do we let this light shine? By being the women that God created us to be, by being women who know, in the depths of our souls, that we are worthy.

Venerable Archbishop Fulton J. Sheen gives us a great insight into the power of women in the world and the influence that we have on history. The power we carry as women who know that we are worthy is formidable, to say the least. Sheen writes,

---

[14] Williamson, Marianne. "A Return to Love." *Marianne Williamson*. Web. <http://www.marianne.com/>.

> "To a great extent the level of any civilization is the level of its womanhood. When a man loves a woman, he has to become worthy of her. The higher her virtue, the more noble her character, the more devoted she is to truth, justice, and goodness, the more a man has to aspire to be worthy of her. The history of civilization could actually be written in terms of the *level of its women.*"[15]

The challenge that lies before us then is to keep the light of worthiness alive. In doing so, we challenge other women to see themselves as worthy, and consequently challenge men to be worthy of us. Thus, as women of worth, we will effectively raise the level of civilization. "Then he [Jesus] said, to all, 'If anyone wishes to come after me he must...take up his cross daily and follow me.'"[16] Come, let us take up our crosses, and with them, let us take up the truth that He finds us worthy.

---

[15] Sheen, Fulton J. "Knowing and Loving." *Life Is Worth Living*. San Franciso: Ignatius, 1999. 61.

[16] Luke 9:23.

Precious Little

For years once I came to believe in God, Proverbs 31 was bantered around as the end-all-be-all for women. I would hear women say things like, "I want to be a Proverbs 31 woman" and men would say, "I want to marry a Proverbs 31 woman, she is the Mary to my Joseph, the Sarah to my Abraham," so on and so forth. It sounded great, so naturally I opened up my Bible to figure out just what it would mean to be a Proverbs 31 woman. I opened my Bible with high hopes because, at long last, the answers were all in my hands, the words were already printed on pages that lay before me just waiting to be read! How glorious it sounded, and how deep my disappointment was.

Allow me to preface: the word of God never disappoints me. I was looking for answers about who a woman of worth is and how I could be like "her", whoever she was. She was the golden calf to my idolatry, so I suppose that it is a good thing I was disappointed. I read Proverbs 31 and after a few verses I was already tired. Proverbs 31 seemed to me to be a long, long checklist of things that any "good and upright" woman or "worthy wife" would do. Instead of feeling empowered to go out and become this mighty and amazing woman, I was left feeling tired, defeated, and unsure that no matter how hard I tried I would ever be anything like the woman described in Proverbs 31. My hopes of discovering what it meant to be a worthy woman, and hopefully someday an ideal wife, had been dashed. I wanted to know about who she is, at her core. I wanted to know what makes up her heart, where her heart rests, and how she finds her strength. For the most part, what I found was a list of things she does. She brings her husband good, not evil, she obtains wool and flax, and she rises while it is still night to distribute food to her household. She picks out fields to purchase, she plants vineyards, she enjoys her successes, she makes her own coverlets, and her husband is prominent at the city gates. She makes clothes and sells them, and the list of things she does goes on and on. Are you tired yet? How does she have time to do all of these things and have a moment to sleep? Oh wait, she doesn't really sleep, she awakes while it is night to put food out! The more I read about this much beloved, highly praised "Proverbs 31 Woman", the less I wanted to be like her. In fact, the more I read about her the more I wanted to yell at her to take a break, she is making the rest of us look bad. Yes, she *does* all of these things, great and wonderful though they may be, but *who is she?* What about her character? What about her heart? Are we to believe that a woman of worth can only be judged and deemed as such by what she does? Is there no merit to her heart?

Shining Verse

Finally, after what felt like forever, I arrived at the verse that made my heart sing. I was tired just thinking about all the things I would have to do to in order to be deemed an ideal wife. I want more about who a woman should *be* and not necessarily so much about the epic list of things she *does*. As Christopher West said, "Holiness is not first a matter of doing anything. It is first and foremost a matter of letting it be done. Holiness is to conceive the love of God within and to bring it forth to the world." Holiness, worthiness, is not first a matter of doing anything! First, something must be done to us: we come to the life-changing realization that we are worthy of unending and unconditional love. Holiness, and I would also contend worthiness, is to conceive the love of God within and then bring it forth to the world. I read Proverbs 31 and can't help but wonder if the only way we bring forth the love of God to the world is through what sounds like the long lists of chores my mother assigned when I was a child.

Then I read verse 25. Proverbs 31:25 held the simple truth that I had been looking for. This chapter was full of things to do but it said precious little about what it means to *be* a woman of worth. Proverbs 31:25 is truly precious, a diamond in the rough, and it has this to say about the woman of worth, "She is clothed with strength and dignity, and she laughs at the days to come." This verse is simple, succinct, and filled with brilliance and wisdom. *Finally*, I thought, something about her character, her heart, and who she is at her core. This verse, in one swift sentence, wraps up what it means to be a worthy woman. This verse teaches us about what it means to live as a worthy woman.

Proverbs 31:25 teaches us a number of things about this woman who is worthy of praise, first among which is that she is clothed. Why stop there? Isn't she clothed with strength and dignity? Yes, and trust me, we will get to those. We can't help but rush past "she is clothed" when we read it and yet there is a simplicity and truth that we miss when we rush past that phrase. She, the woman who is deemed to be an ideal wife, the cream of the crop, the holy grail of women is clothed, plain and simple.

Alluring and Transcendent

There is something mysterious and alluring about a woman when she is covered up. I'm not saying you need to dump your whole wardrobe, buy a habit and only wear that, but women should be clothed. We as women - single or not - have a certain power or sway over men by the way we dress. Put on a tiny skirt, go out in public, and you will be tempting other people, men and women, to see you as a thing rather than a person. Go to the beach in your bikini if you must, but please don't act surprised when you hear guys whistling at you and checking you out. Most girls I know wouldn't go parading around town in their bra and underwear because that's just not the way to dress and inspire respect. Why is your bikini any different simply because it is a different kind of material? It hardly leaves anything to the imagination.

Remember the quote from Archbishop Fulton J. Sheen about women determining the level of civilization? If you sell yourself short by not keeping your standards high and respecting your own body then guys are not challenged to be a man worthy of such a noble woman. We determine the level of civilization by the way we act and the way we dress. Pretty women inspire and challenge men to truly be men, and godly, holy men at that. Recall the article "The Death of Pretty". In it, Pat Archbold states, "That special combination of beauty and innocence, the pretty inspires men to protect and defend it."[17] Make no mistake, it is not that we are weak damsels in distress in dire need of being rescued, but when we respect ourselves enough to espouse modesty, we inspire boys to be men. We can, by the way we dress, inspire men to stand up, and, if and when the time comes, defend us, our

---

[17] Archbold, Pat. "The Death of Pretty." *National Catholic Register*. EWTN News, 21 Dec. 2011. Web. <http://www.ncregister.com/blog/the-death-of-pretty>.

honor, our natural beauty, and our dignity. There isn't a woman I know who doesn't want that kind of quality in a man.

Do you remember Danny Zuko in *Grease*? He sees the innocence, the beauty and the wonder of Sandy and he is inspired by her. Over the course of the musical he becomes so inspired by her beauty that he changes for the better. He trades in his rebel ways and becomes a clean-cut do-gooder. That doesn't mean that to be a man a guy has to trade in his leather jacket for a letterman's jacket and become the preppy kid next door. However, Sandy's beauty and modesty inspire Danny to leave his boyish days of chasing girls behind for the honor of being her man and defending her beauty. Archbold continues,

> "Young women today do not seem to aspire to pretty, they prefer to be regarded as hot...something altogether different. When women want to be hot instead of pretty, they must view themselves in a certain way...As I said, pretty inspires men's nobler instincts to protect and defend. Pretty is cherished. Hotness, on the other hand, is a commodity. Its value is temporary and must be used."[18]

Would you rather be a commodity or be cherished? Would you rather be cared for tenderly or used? Blessed Pope John Paul II taught that the opposite of love is not hatred, it is use.[19] When we use another person we fail to value them and respect them for the person God created them to be. In so using them we also give them permission to treat us in the same way, without the respect, honor, or dignity we were created for.

---

[18] Ibid.

[19] cf. Wojtyla, Karol. *Love and Responsibility*. San Francisco: Ignatius, 1993.

The question remains, would you rather be loved or used? Isn't that like asking would you rather live in a palace and feast, or live in a box in the streets and starve? Isn't the answer obvious? Our hearts were made for the feast at the palace, and our bodies image the God who created us, the God who lives eternally in the Palace of Heaven, whose feast never ends. Why, then, do we sell ourselves short and live in a box on the streets and starve when the feast of Heaven awaits us? We were made for more; we were made for and in the image of Beauty. There is something to be said for being pretty versus being hot. Heat is fleeting, it can turn cold over time, but beauty is eternal. Beauty is transcendent and is not limited by time or space. Imagine your favorite painting or photograph, or perhaps even your favorite place to watch the sunset. Isn't the beauty of any one of those things transcendent? I think of my favorite place to watch the sunset and even if I am not there to take in the sunset, the beauty of that place remains intact. The beauty of that place is not dependent on someone appreciating it, the beauty of that place simply *is*. Beauty comes from within, and it reflects the beauty of its Creator, just as we are called to let the beauty that is within us shine and reflect the beauty of that same Creator.

There comes a time in most women's lives when they want to be regarded as "hot" because, ironically enough, being "hot" is the "cool" thing to be. I've had a number of conversations over the years with ladies who want to be regarded as either hot or beautiful. The women I have talked to who want to be seen as beautiful have often already experienced a time in their lives when they wanted to be seen as hot, but the time has come when they don't miss those days. Most women wish they could have the days of being hot back because they have come to the realization that being hot is a fleeting and subjective notion; they recognize that the truest kind of beauty comes from within. So what is the difference between being hot and being beautiful? We look at women who desire to be hot and we feel sorry for them in some sense because we know that they are selling themselves short. Women who aspire to be hot sell themselves short in many ways, but one of the clearest ways they sell themselves short is in the way they dress.

Watch any reality TV dating show and you'll see what I mean. Even if you only watch the first episode where the participants meet each other, you'll be struck by the lack of clothing worn by the girls who want to be seen as hot. Low-cut dresses that allow cleavage to flow about and be seen by everyone are all the rage. Silly and ditzy laughs at even the dumbest things will apparently make you hot as well. If, perhaps, the first two things aren't working, feel free to try a short dress on, the ones that barely cover what they need to cover when you are standing up, and God only knows what happens to that "dress" when you sit down. Chances are that if you are tugging and pulling at your skirt or dress to get it to stay up or down, or both, then it is not an appropriate piece of clothing for a woman of worth. Apparently the motto of women trying to be hot is, "because I'm so hot, I need to wear less clothing to compensate." What a sad motto it is.

Archbold accurately points out that hotness is a commodity, one that is temporary and must be used. Think of what you use in your everyday life: a computer, your cell phone, your blow-dryer, etc. They are all *things*. We use things; we are not supposed to use people. Much of the troubles we face in the world today are because we've begun to love things and use people, rather than loving people and using things. People are called to be loved, not used, not consumed and thrown away like yesterday's newspaper. Don't sell yourself short and certainly don't sell God's creation – you – short either. Clothe yourself for goodness sake; clothe yourself so that you may be regarded as beautiful, as a person and a woman who reflects the beauty of her Creator. Clothe your body so that the beauty of your soul can shine. As Saint Ambrose wrote, "You soul must hold fast to Him, you must follow after Him in your thoughts, you must tread His ways by faith, not in outward show." Allow your soul to cling to Him and follow after Him and the beauty that you were created for will radiate from within you.

Beauty

There is no recipe for beauty, and it looks different for every woman. Take the time to find what makes you beautiful, the answer lives within you. In high school I wrote journal entries which I called "I Found What Makes Me Beautiful", and each of them contained something different that I felt made me beautiful. Beauty isn't dependent on someone appreciating it, but rather true beauty comes from within. As Elizabeth Kubler-Ross once said, "People are like stained glass windows. They sparkle and shine when the sun is out, but when the darkness sets in, their true beauty is revealed only if there is a light from within." When the darkness sets in – and it will – we have to remember that there is a light within us. One of the things I wrote about in high school was that what made me beautiful was surrender to God. By surrendering to God all of my worries, plans, and concerns I was free and that freedom radiated within me. I felt beautiful because I wasn't weighed down by worry or concern. To some degree, that is still true, and surrendering everything, and I do mean *everything* to God, makes me feel beautiful because I allow Him to fill me with His love. When anyone is filled with the love of God I hardly think there could be anything or anyone more beautiful. I think of Blessed Mother Teresa or Blessed Pope John Paul II and how emptied they were of their own concerns about life, and yet how full of the love of God they were, and how much that love radiate to others. By most people's standards those two may not be beautiful. They may never have been on the cover of the magazine as the sexiest man or woman of the year and yet they were undeniably beautiful because their beauty imaged the divine, and what could be more beautiful than that?

As I've grown up I have realized that there are different things that make me beautiful. Going without makeup makes me feel beautiful. Some days it is harder than others and I would love to just put some eye liner on, but going without makeup not only saves me money, but it challenges me to appreciate the beauty that God created in me, just as He created it. By going without makeup I have slowly given up some of the vanities that once paralyzed me, and there is something sacred about seeing God when you look in the mirror and knowing that He created you just as you are. There is a simplistic wonder in knowing that He loves you, even, and perhaps especially without makeup on. Think of the Virgin Mary; would she be any more beautiful if she had worn mascara or blush? I should think not. She was filled with and consumed by the love of God and she was undeniably beautiful.

Spending time in nature also makes me feel beautiful. I see God's wonderful imagination in His created world and I recognize that the same genius He used to create the mountains and the oceans He also used when He created me. In our bodies and souls we reflect the artistic genius of the God who created the beauty that we find in nature. His beauty lives within us. I feel beautiful going to a store and trying on fancy ball gowns. I feel beautiful when I can cry. It took me many years to be able to cry in front of or around anyone. When I'm being honest and vulnerable, whether it is with a good sister in Christ or alone in a church, I feel beautiful. Vulnerability is beautiful. There are different things that make each of us feel beautiful and it is vitally important to who we are as worthy women to find those things and hold on to them. Beauty comes from within.

"The City of Blinding Lights" by U2 often comes to mind when I think about being beautiful. In it Bono repeatedly sings about how beautiful the character of the song is. Each time he sings it you can hear the passion in his voice, and you can hear how stunned and taken aback he is by the beauty that he sings of. The words of that simple phrase don't just flow out, there is a pause between each word as if he has to catch his breath because the beauty that he sees is that awe-inspiring. Isn't that the kind of passion you would want to hear? God already has that kind of passion for you and He tells you that every day. Wouldn't you rather hear "Oh, you look so beautiful tonight" instead of "Oh you look so hot tonight"? Beauty is transcendent and eternal; heat is fleeting and temporary, and must be used and consumed. Beauty inspires and challenges, it is loved and adored, never used and consumed. Beauty is appreciated, upheld, defended, and honored. Hotness simply is not. Whether it is an earthly man or the God of the Universe I would much rather hear that I am beautiful tonight, today, and every day.

Bono goes on to sing that he misses the beauty when it – city, woman, child, whoever or whatever – is not around. Beauty is missed, hotness is absorbed and forgotten about. Beauty is sought after, hotness is not. Bono, in the sight of this beauty, wonders, if the beauty can see the beauty within him. He wonders what happened to the beauty he had inside of him. We want others to see our beauty, or rather, the beauty of God inside of us. We wonder if others can see that beauty in us and we hope that the light of beauty within us shines brightly enough to be seen. In the sight of a great beauty one can't help but notice when beauty has faded within our own hearts, and it sends us on a quest to find that beauty, rediscover it, and let it shine. We behold a great beauty, such as God and His created world, and we are sent on our own quest to hold such a great beauty within us and share it with others. Beauty in one woman or man has the ability to light a fire for it within another.

Finally, Bono concludes that time will not leave him as he is, and that time can't take the boy out of the man. Then, once again, Bono sings of the beauty of the character of the song. Time never leaves us as we are, it always changes us. Time, however, can't take a boy and turn him into a man. Conversely, beauty has the power and the influence to take the boy out of the man. Beauty can change a boy into a man, one who defends and honors all of God's creation.

C.S. Lewis writes about the power of beauty in *The Weight of Glory*, noting,

> "We do not want to merely see beauty, though, God knows, even that is bounty enough. We want something else which can hardly be put into words – to be united with the beauty we see, to pass into it, to receive it into ourselves, to bathe in it, to become part of it."[20]

We long for the transcendental beauty we were made from. We reflect this beauty, so it is no wonder that we desire to be united with another's beauty. This is exactly why beauty inspires: we want to be united with the God whose beauty we were created from. We want to enter into beauty just as we yearn for beautiful sunsets, blooming flowers in the spring, and the first snowfall. We want to bathe in beauty and become a part of it. In our modesty we invite others to become a part of the beauty that God has gifted us with. The world tries to sell us on countless products, thinking that they will make us more beautiful. What we fail to realize, however, is that God's beauty is already within us, begging to be appreciated and adored. We espouse modesty so that our souls, filled with the love of Christ, may shine, inviting others to become a part of unending beauty.

If you want to be a real woman, a godly woman, espouse modesty. As the old adage goes, your clothing should be tight

---

[20] Lewis, C. S. *The Weight of Glory*. New York: Harper One, 1980. 42.

enough to show that you are a woman, but loose enough to show you are a lady. If you want to attract a guy, or perhaps more accurately a boy, then by all means aspire to be hot. But I can almost guarantee you that in his eyes, your hotness will fade and he'll quickly move on to some other "hot" thing, not a hot person, and there is quite a difference. If you want to dress scantily and be noticed for your lack of clothing no one is stopping you. However, I would be willing to bet that if you dress in that way, the kind of attention you will receive isn't actually the kind of attention your heart truly desires. Chances are that if a man sees your beauty, a beauty that comes from the self-confidence that allows you to say (more with your choice of clothes than your mouth), "There is a beauty that comes from within me, there is something mysterious and intriguing about me; I don't need to lower my standards in any way, especially by showing you most of my skin just to attract your superficial and fleeting attention", then he'll stick around and his attraction to you will be deeper than your looks.

Clothing yourself in imitation of the woman described in Proverbs 31 allows you to convey that you are interested in more than fleeting glances and hooking up, it says that what is most important to you is your heart, and the God that makes His home within it. When we allow God to dwell in our hearts it is His beauty that makes us beautiful. Whether or not we feel ready to be on the cover of a magazine, when we see that God sees us as beautiful, we begin to believe it too. Clothing yourself, covering yourself up doesn't say "I'm ugly" or "I don't think I'm hot", nor does it say "I want to be a nun someday", but rather it says, "I'm something worth fighting for - I'm a rarity in the world today and I value myself as a person, not just an object to be used and thrown away." God sees us as a rarity in the world, and He knows our rarity better than anyone else. He passionately desires for us to see the rare and radiant beauty He created in each and every one of us.

Think of what is rare and precious in the world: diamonds, gold, silver, pearls, rubies, sapphires - beautiful things and precious stones. The things that are rare and precious in the world are things or items that are seen, sought after, pursued, and are worth the quest and the struggle to acquire them. Jewelers and collectors all over the world pay top dollar for what is rare because they want to hold on to and appreciate beauty. Miners pan for gold and spend hours, days, weeks, and years searching through mud and river water in hopes of finding gold and silver. True beauty is sought after with passion and purpose, even in muddy and dirty river water because the prize – the beauty – is worth the search.

Think of what is commonplace in the world: plastic, paper, yarn, string. The rare and precious things are sought after and adored. Gollum, in the *Lord of the Rings* seeks after "my precious" with all that he is because he deems it beautiful, and its allure consumes him. The beauty of the ring speaks to Gollum and he can hardly stand to be parted from his precious. On the contrary, the commonplace things are fleeting and are thrown away with yesterday's news. As far as I can remember there has never been a great plastic rush. There have, on the other hand, been gold rushes. People search for and pursue that which is rare and precious. God created you to be rare and precious. God created you for glory, allow yourself to be sought after and pursued.

Strength

The more I've prayed about it the more I've come to realize that we weren't necessarily made to be strong as women, or as people. The strength we have as women is radically different than most people would think. I am, by no stretch of the imagination, saying that women or people in general were created to be weak. What I do know is what Saint Paul tells us about God's power and strength in his second letter to the church in Corinth, "My grace is sufficient for you, for power is made perfect in weakness."[1] God's power is perfect all on its own; it doesn't need our weakness to be perfect. What Paul is telling us is that we see the perfection of God's strength and power in our own weakness. When I find that I am feeling superbly weak, it is then that I find the grace and perfection of God's infinite strength. I would far rather see God's strength brought to perfection in my weakness than feel the need to be strong all the time. Being strong all the time is tiring; let Him shoulder the load with us.

Saint Paul goes on to write, "I will rather boast most gladly of my weaknesses, in order that the power of Christ may dwell with me. Therefore, I am content with weaknesses...for the sake of Christ; for when I am weak, then I am strong."[2] The world today tells us a far different story. The world tells us to be strong, rub some dirt on it, don't cry, quitting is for sissies, walking away is cowardly, so on and so forth. Weakness today is certainly nothing to boast about. Just had your heart broken? So what, the world says, put on a happy face and go to work. Lost your job and can't

---

[1] 2 Corinthians 12:9.

[2] 2 Corinthians 12:9-10.

pay your bills? Too bad, so sad, you won't find any pity, sympathy, much less empathy, anywhere around here. Suffered a death in the family? Well, okay, you can have two days bereavement leave, but no more. Oh and when you return to work you better look your best and not cry all the time, or at all, for that matter. Weakness is something altogether rejected by the world today. The world says we are to embrace strength and put on a strong and rugged exterior no matter how broken our insides are. Even Proverbs 31:25 says that the woman of worth is clothed with strength and dignity. I would contend, however, that the strength that Proverbs speaks of is far different from the strength the world espouses today. The world calls us to put on a brave face, no matter how broken we may be. In the end, the strength that the world asks of us only leaves us broken and jaded, because we are pretending to be something we are not, we are living inauthentic lives. True strength comes from being weak, just as the apostle Paul was. To be weak is to be beautiful, vulnerable, tender, real, and unabashedly honest. Anyone who tells you anything different is lying to you, afraid to be weak themselves, thinks they don't need God, or all of the above. Paul boasted of his weakness and was filled with the strength of God. Open your heart, especially to God, even if it is the most daunting thing you do, so that God, who is Love, may enter in. Paul boasted of his weakness and found strength in God, should we not also follow after his example, and boast in our weaknesses so that God may fill us with His strength?

The Irony of It All

The irony is that being weak actually helps us to be strong, because by being weak, by admitting our faults and our shortcomings, we are able to depend more fully on Him, the source of infinite strength. As women of worth, we are called to be clothed with strength, which actually means that we are clothed in His strength.

Think about what happens in your life and your heart after a break-up. I'm not talking about a dramatic break-up, I'm talking about a break-up from someone you truly loved and felt called to be with and then it simply ends. The pain in your heart is real, tangible, and nearly overwhelming. So where do we find the strength to get out of bed? To go to work? To talk to people? We find it in Him. When we are weak our hearts cry out – whether it is a conscious cry or not – that we don't know how to do this on our own and we aren't sure how to carry on. It is the painfully honest cry of our hearts that God hears and He comes to comfort and strengthen His daughters. He comes, as Psalm 91 says, to "rescue you from the fowler's snare, from the destroying plague, [God] will shelter you with pinions, spread wings that you may take refuge; God's faithfulness is a protecting shield."[3] God will shelter you because His faithfulness is a protecting shield. He wraps the whole wing around you as He keeps you safe and sheltered under His enormous wingspan. When our hearts cry out to Him, He comes with the mighty love of a Father to guard us in the safety of His wings.

I think back on the break-ups I have gone through and wonder how I ever made it out of bed the next day, or ever returned to work when I felt as though I had nothing left in me. That is not to say that I had based my sense of self-worth on the

---

[3] Psalm 91:3-4.

guy I was with, but rather that I had invested myself in the relationships and had my heart broken. Anyone who has ever had a broken heart knows how painful it can be to carry on in the aftermath of it all. Any strength I found in those hours, days, and weeks after the break-ups came from God wrapping His arms around me – whether I knew He was doing so or not. The strength we find in those times we are weak – after a break up, the death of a loved one, or a blow to our career – comes not from our own hearts but rather from the One who dwells in our hearts.

The other place we find strength in times of weakness is from those we trust and love, those special friends and family members God has placed in our lives for a reason. Miraculously, we draw not only from His strength which lives in our hearts, but we also draw strength from the strength He shares with the people around us. We find comfort and solace, peace and strength in the fellowship we share with others. He fills up His children not only so that they themselves may be filled but also so that they can share His strength with His children who feel as though they lack it. Our cups overflow so that others may be filled through our overabundance of strength and love. Saint Bernard of Clairvaux once wrote, "If then you are wise, you will show yourself rather as a reservoir than as a canal. A canal spreads abroad water as it receives it, but a reservoir waits until it is filled before overflowing, and thus without loss to itself [it shares] its superabundant water."[4] God calls us to be reservoirs so that we may fill each other up.

---

[4] Clairvaux, Bernard of. *Life and Works of Saint Bernard, Abbot of Clairvaux*. Ed. Jean Mabillon and Samuel J. Eales. London: J. Hodges, 1889. 101.

The phrase "help me..." is the most common phrase you will find in my journals and prayers for good reason. I need help. We need help. We find our strength in Him because we can't carry the load on our own. There is nothing humiliating or shameful about accepting help when the load becomes too much for us to carry. Even Jesus, the Son of God, accepted the help of Simon the Cyrene on the way to Golgotha. The cross was too heavy for Jesus to carry Himself. He was not too proud to accept help. It took true strength for Jesus to admit that He couldn't go it alone. Jesus showed us that when we are weak, when we are lost and doubting, we not only should ask for help to carry the crosses that life gives us, we need to accept help. If we open our eyes to it we see that the Source of strength gives us many channels to grow in strength. Though His strength and the strength of the Simons of Cyrene in our lives we are invited to constantly draw from His strength.

There are many great writers and theologians who have written about what it means to depend on God and find our strength in Him. My favorite quotes and thoughts about God's strength and our need of it come from C.S. Lewis. He writes,

> "The thing is to rely *only* on God. The time will come when you will regard all this misery as a small price to pay for having been brought to that dependence. Meanwhile, the trouble is that relying on God has to begin all over again every day as if nothing has yet been done."[5]

---

[5] Lewis, Clive Staples, and Warren Hamilton. Lewis. *Letters of C. S. Lewis: Edited with a Memoir by W. H. Lewis.* London: G. Bles, 1966. 395.

The thing is to rely on God for *everything*, first and foremost. Rely on Him for strength, love, hope, purpose, meaning, life, your own worth, comfort, and for reassurance. When we depend on other people first for any of those things we begin to love God less and those people more, thus slipping into idolatry. Lewis knew that he had to love God as he ought to before he could love his earthly dearest or else it would lead to demise; Lewis wrote, "In so far as I learn to love my earthly dearest at the expense of God and instead of God...I shall not love my earthly dearest at all. When first things are put first, second things are not suppressed but increased."[6] We rely first on God. We have come to see that in this battle of life that such a dependence on God is not easy and, fittingly, Lewis goes so far as to call it misery.

There are days I feel like a dog with a collar wrapped around my neck tied to a dog house. I see something beautiful and shiny and try to run at it and find myself being yanked backwards, bewildered as to why I can't run. God, in this metaphor, is the dog house. I find myself trying to be satisfied and find strength in relationships or in my job or all on my own and He continually yanks me back to Him. As the prophet Hosea puts it,

> "Therefore, I will hedge in her way with thorns and erect a wall against her, so that she cannot find her paths. If she runs after her lovers, she shall not overtake them; if she looks for them she shall not find them. Then she shall say, 'I will go back to my first husband, for it was better with me then than now.'"[7]

---

[6] Lewis, C.S., and Sigmund Freud. Ed. Armand M. Nicholi. *The Question of God: C.S. Lewis and Sigmund Freud Debate God, Love, Sex, and the Meaning of Life*. New York: Free, 2002. 106.

Perhaps this sounds cruel of God to do, hedge in our way with thorns and build a wall up against us, but in fact it is quite the opposite. Such action is filled with love because He prevents us from being hurt by others through an invitation to a deeper dependence on Him. He asks us to build a foundation of strength on His own strength and then He shall take down the walls that we have built up around our hearts. Eventually we come to a point, weakened by the struggle of trying to break free from the collar that ties us to the doghouse, and we submit to God saying, "I will come back to You, it is far better with You than it could ever be anywhere else." We are the dog and God is the dog house, constantly calling us to come home and depend on His strength. The reward for such dependence is beyond measure – peace, joy, happiness, love, and eventually, Heaven. The miserable truth is that such work must begin again every day as if we had done nothing towards such dependence before. The work begins over and over, every single day. We have two choices then: be miserable about constantly starting over, or see each day as an opportunity to improve and come to a greater dependence on Him in all that we do. After all, Lewis concludes, "To what will you look for help if not to that which is stronger than yourself?"[8]

Vulnerability

The beautiful thing about loving God is that there is no vulnerability with Him. Being vulnerable implies some risk, some uncertainty in the relationship. We may be uncertain at times of

---

[7] Hosea 2:8-9.

[8] Lewis, C.S. *The Complete C.S. Lewis Signature Classics*. [San Francisco, Calif.]: HarperSanFrancisco, 2002. 56.

what God is asking of us, but there is no uncertainty in His love for us. In fact, God loves your vulnerability. The idea of it sounds odd at first, but God loves you pouring your heart out to Him. No matter how angry we are at Him or how hurt we are, He can take it all. So why pour out our hearts to God if He already knows what is in them? Because it is often in the pouring out of our hearts that we discover what is there in the first place.

Have you ever been in a really bad fight with someone, your sister, your mother, your best friend, or your significant other? You go on yelling and when you really get fighting the painful words come out, it is virtually inevitable. Sometimes in letting it all out, in letting God have it, we finally see what the core issue is and what has been bothering us so much in the first place. There are times that I go into a church and find that it is empty. In those precious moments alone with God I pour my heart out. I speak out loud. I sing, even if it is off-pitch. I cry like a baby. I say whatever pops into my head, no matter how painful or hurtful it may be. In those moments of complete openness with God He almost always leads me to see what has been in front of my eyes for so long. God loves our vulnerability because it frees us, it allows us to breathe, to see ourselves – and His love – from a different perspective. By pouring our hearts out, by emptying ourselves of all our burdens we make room for Him to fill us with His love and strength.

Our strength as women comes not so much from putting on the rugged exterior, cleaning the house, walking the dog, doing the chores, holding down a job, raising a family, etc. Rather, our strength is a quieter, more calm and steady strength. The strength of a man and the strength of a woman are very different, and yet both reflect the strength of God. When I think of strong men I think of men who have experienced the trials of life and still hold fast to their faith. I think of good family men who love their wives, are faithful to their marriage vows and, in time, are good role models to their children. A strong man is one who is rugged, who has a wild heart that is filled with passion for whatever the Lord calls him to. The strength of men is evident, not necessarily in the way they look, but in the way they conduct themselves and live their lives. The strength of a woman is quite different, and yet so necessary.

Guys I know often think that a woman is strong if she displays a strong sense of who she is, what her values are, what is acceptable in life and what is not. Perhaps this is true, but I would contend that the strength of a woman runs much deeper. A woman's strength is revealed when she lets her walls down, when she drops her guard and shares her tender heart with others. Let's face it: we have been guarded since The Fall. We are afraid to hope for eternity, even though our soul longs for it. We are afraid to trust Adam, who stood there in silence as God questioned us, and when he did speak, he simply pointed the finger at us. We are guarded. Even if we weren't there in the Garden of Eden we still have our reasons to be guarded. Heart break, disappointment, feeling unloved, unnoticed, suffering through the deaths of loved ones, and all the tragedies of life have taught us to be guarded. Women show strength by letting those walls down. It takes more strength than most guys can imagine to let down the walls that guard our hearts and let anyone in. We show our strength by being vulnerable, with each other, with our significant others, with our families, and with God.

For most women I know putting on that outwardly strong face is the easiest thing they do in a day. We can put it on, go to work and make it seem like everything is fine, even when our hearts are broken from the trials of life. Our real strength is shown in fellowship, when we let trusted people into our hearts. Our strength is shown when we cry. Our strength is shown when we allow others to see our brokenness and no longer hide behind the walls that guard our hearts. True strength for a woman is our ability to be vulnerable. We first start by being vulnerable with God, by allowing Him into our hearts, no matter how broken they may be. Then we can begin to let others in, our family, our friends, our significant others, and we hope and pray that they come to realize that we were not strong before when we put on the brave face, but now we are because we can admit that we are weak and in need of help. To most people this notion of being strong by admitting we are weak makes no sense, and yet to those who know Christ this notion makes perfect sense. Christ was weakened beneath the weight of the cross and the more He poured out His heart to His Father, the more God the Father strengthened Jesus. The more emptied we are of ourselves the more we can be filled with Him. Think of the religious who are cloistered, monks who live in community, and the desert fathers, they are all emptied of themselves and beautifully filled with His love and His radiance. To admit that we are weak or that we are lost or confused or heartbroken, or to admit that we have wounds from this battle of life is to admit that we need God. Admitting that we need God is the most beautiful place we can be, and it is the most hopeful place we can be. When life knocks you down to your knees remember that you are in the perfect position to pray. Admission of need for Him is the beginning of a beautiful journey of love, hope, peace and strength. Weakness and pride cannot coexist. Admitting that we are weak means we must rid ourselves of pride – the greatest force keeping us from God – and ask for help.

Our tender vulnerability speaks to the tender strength of God. Just as a man's strength speaks to the rugged and wild heart of God, so too the female's strength speaks to the tender and compassionate heart of God. God showed us His strength by sending Jesus to die for us, by being humiliated on the cross and laying down His life for us. Could He have been any more vulnerable with us? Men's and women's strength complement each other because both come from the heart of God. Sometimes it is hard for us to appreciate the strength of men because we want them to open up to us and share their souls with us and be more vulnerable. Sometimes it is hard for men to appreciate our strength because they want us to suck it up and put on that brave face they once saw us with. But we weren't made that way, and neither were men. We were made for each other, to be vulnerable with each other and to protect each other. There is no vulnerability in loving God because all of our other relationships are filled with it, which is exactly why we cling to His love beyond all others. The strength of a woman is an inner strength, quiet and peaceful as she invites you in to her heart, no matter how broken or wounded it may be. Such inner feminine strength only comes from depending on Him above all else and opening our hearts to Him first.

Whenever I am struggling to admit that I am weak and in need of help, in need of His strength, two songs come to mind. Both renew my hope in His love and comfort me in my weakness. The first song, "Carry Me Through" by Dave Barnes, is about the times in life that we feel there is a mountain before us, a struggle too large to face on our own. Barnes sings that he will climb it, but with a strength that is not his own, because he knows that God will meet him where the mountains beat him, and that God will carry him through. No matter how high the mountains of life are, He will meet us exactly where it beats us and He will carry us through. Always. Every time. No matter what. Barnes continues with a simple prayer that the Lord would be gentle with us and remember that we are human. He hopes that God won't crush us and that God will recall how hard we try. Our hearts cry out to God in our weakness. When we reach the point that we can admit that we are weak, we still hope and pray that He won't crush us, and we want to remind Him that we've tried so hard. We continue to walk tall, not on our own, but by His grace. Rest assured that He sees our efforts and that His loving, tender, compassionate and empathetic heart is coming to heal us and fill us with His strength. He comes to lift us up, help us carry our crosses, and unite our struggles to Jesus'. It has been said that God does not give us more than we can handle, but I think that He gives us more than we can handle on our own so that we learn to give some, if not all, of our struggles back to Him and so find our strength to carry on with Him.

The second song that comes to mind is "Savior, Please" by Josh Wilson. He sings that we do the best we can, but we don't know how long we can persevere alone. We recognize that we need God to hold on to us because we know that we are nothing without His love. So it is that we ask our Savior to continue to save us. The sentiments are the same because we all struggle with feeling weak. I have yet to meet a person who never thought they had a weak moment in their life. We can't do this alone; we need God to hold on to us. We need Him to keep saving us and to keep filling us with His strength. Wilson continues, asking the Savior to help him stand, and acknowledges that we fall so hard and we fade so quickly. We ask God to begin at the exact place where we end because we need Him to be the God of all that we are because He is all that we have. We continue to find that we are being yanked by our collars back to the dog house. We chase after lovers that don't satisfy. We pursue gods that are not God. The answer to all of our questions is yes, God will begin right where we end. He will meet us where the mountain beats us and He will be the God of all that we are, if only we let Him. Our strength as women starts and ends with our own vulnerability with God. Rest your heart, tender, weak, beautiful, broken, scarred, and loved with God, and there you will find His strength filling you to become a reservoir of strength.

Fight the Good Fight

As Dostoevsky once wrote, "God and the devil are fighting...and the battlefield is the heart of man."[9] The truth of the matter is that we need God's strength because there is a battle

---

[9] Dostoevsky, Fyodor. *The Brothers Karamozov*. Macmillan, 1922. 110.

under way. The battle is for our souls and this battle has been going on since the beginning of time. Therefore, we need God's strength to reside in our hearts and fill us with courage because the spiritual battles are afoot and our only hope of victory and of saving our own souls (and others' souls) is found in Him. Satan must be defeated, lest we die in the coffins in which he seeks to lock us away.

Satan has many tools in his arsenal against us. He, if you will remember, is the Father of Lies; he has no good tricks up his sleeve. It is not that Satan really wants you to himself, but he certainly does not want you to be God's. Satan will stop at nothing – short of the power of God – to keep your soul from God. Satan's two most powerful weapons come in the form of thoughts we ascribe to, or ideas that we come to believe over time. The first is, "Satan doesn't have the power to attack me" and the second is, "Who am I that Satan would come after me?" Bam. You, probably without realizing it, have just given Satan more power than you would ever consciously, willingly give him.

The first thought that gives Satan power may not seem all that threatening. Surely Satan doesn't really have *power*. Theologians have debated this point for years and the jury is still debating. However, Satan certainly has sway, persuasion and a cunning ability to get inside our heads. Saying that Satan doesn't have power is like looking at a giant line-backer for a football team and saying that he can't hurt you. Saying that Satan, who was once the most loved of all the angels, doesn't have power is like standing before the Great Wall of China and calling it small. When we sell someone short of their potential it only gives them more drive to prove us wrong. Hasn't anyone ever told you that you weren't good enough, smart enough, or pretty enough? Doesn't that statement on some level make you want to prove them wrong? The same is true of Satan. Sit here and think to yourself, or worse, tell other people that Satan doesn't have power and he'll do everything he can to prove you wrong.

What is perhaps worse than selling Satan's power short is selling your own worth short. By thinking that you aren't worth Satan's time you begin to believe that he won't ever attack you or try to sway you away from God, not to mention the fact that you don't believe in your own worth. Through that thought Satan has already lulled you into a false sense of security. There, thinking that you are secure, he can attack you without so much as a second thought on your part because you already believe he isn't coming after you. Wake up. *Wake up.* ***<u>WAKE UP.</u>*** You are a child of God. Satan hates God, why would he not come after you, a precious child of God made in God's own image? Just as you begin to think you might be worth something to God or anyone else Satan comes after you, sometimes in obvious ways and sometimes in sneaky ways. If you want some insight as to how Satan and his minions can trick and deceive us, read *The Screwtape Letters* by C.S. Lewis. Lewis captures, in haunting detail, how easily we can be turned and swayed if we aren't careful and aware of what Satan has the ability to do in our lives. The truth is that you are worthy and the second you begin to believe that truth Satan will sit up and take notice and fight to keep you from believing in your own worth. The last thing that Satan wants is for you to hold fast to your own worthiness.

The biggest mistake you can make and the most power you can give to Satan is to think that he simply doesn't exist. In that thought you give him unlimited power because if we believe he doesn't exist then we believe he can't hurt us. We can't be harmed by something or someone that doesn't exist. You don't just get to ignore Satan because you don't like him; it only gives him more power. John Eldredge sums it up quite well when he writes,

> "To live in ignorance of spiritual warfare is the most naïve and dangerous thing a person can do. It's like skipping through the worst part of town, late at night, waving your wallet above your head...It's like swimming with great white sharks, dressed as a wounded sea lion and smeared with blood. And let me tell you something: you don't escape spiritual warfare simply because you choose not to believe it exists or because you refuse to fight it."[10]

The battle is underway, the guns are loaded and the ammunition is plentiful. This is a time of war and you simply can't ignore it because by ignoring it you are risking your soul. Our tender strength is needed in this battle. We, as women, are *needed*, and desperately. Satan would love nothing more than for you to laugh at that. Who are you to be needed? You are a child of God, a woman who is worthy of love, a woman who is coming to know that truth and is allowing the light of God to shine through her. <u>Satan fears you</u>. Satan fears your wonderful, strong, tender, compassionate heart. But as Eldredge concludes, "The bottom

---

[10] Eldredge, John. *Waking the Dead: The Glory of a Heart Fully Alive*. Nashville, TN: Thomas Nelson, 2003. 152.

line is, *you are going to have to fight for your heart.*"[11] The battle is underway, but take courage dear sisters, God has given us weapons and ammunition aplenty so that we can fight the good fight and never allow Satan to win over our souls. The time is now. Are you ready to fight?

Weapons Ready

This is not a battle fought in the trenches. This is not a battle fought by pushing a button and waiting for the bomb to explode on your opponent. This is a battle fought on the front lines, with God valiantly marching before us. This is the most difficult battle because it is the battle for the most important thing in the world: your soul. John Eldredge writes, "Your heart is good. Your heart matters to God. These are the two hardest things to hold on to."[12] Yet hold on to them we must or else we'll lose the battle before it has begun. Despite the gravity of the situation before us, we are not left orphans and we are not left empty-handed. Filled with the strength of God we can stand and fight.

We already know that Satan has weapons he tries to use against us. They are many and often terrifying. We, however, are not without weapons in our fight against him. Our greatest weapon is prayer. It sounds so simple because we all too often underestimate its power. As the *Catechism* details, "In communion with their Master, the disciples' prayer is a battle; only by keeping watch in prayer can one avoid falling into temptation."[13] Prayer engages us in the battle; it awakens us and keeps us alert. Upon

---

[11] Ibid, emphasis added.

[12] Ibid, 153.

[13] CCC 2612

entering the Garden of Gethsemane Jesus encouraged His disciples, "Pray that you may not undergo the test."[14] As we know, the disciples fell asleep while Jesus was praying. Jesus was praying so fervently that his sweat could be likened to blood. And yet, in the Gospel of Luke we read, "To strengthen him an angel from heaven appeared to him."[15] Jesus returned to His disciples and found them sleeping and again encouraged them to pray so that they may not undergo the test.[16] Prayer keeps us awake, alert, and focused on the One who gives us strength. Jesus prayed so fervently and in turn was strengthened when the angel appeared to Him. By entering in to constant prayer we too can be awake, focused on God and strengthened by Him.

There are countless prayers written by the saints throughout the ages that pack such a spiritual punch with them that I would hate to ever be on the receiving end of them. The first one that comes to mind is commonly referred to as the St. Michael the Archangel prayer. Saint Michael is seen as the defender and protector of Heaven. He is always pictured as a strong, valiant warrior and usually is crushing something or someone, typically a demon, under his foot. If I were going into battle I would want Saint Michael by my side. The prayer is known by a few different translations and wordings but goes something like this, "Saint Michael the Archangel, defend us in battle; be our protection against the wickedness and snares of the devil. May God rebuke him, we humbly pray: and do thou, O Prince of the heavenly host,

---

[14] Luke 22:40.

[15] Luke 22:43.

[16] Luke 22:46.

by the power of God, thrust into hell Satan and all the evil spirits who prowl about the world seeking the ruin of souls."

Just reading that makes me shiver. We ask for Saint Michael's intercession and that he would defend us in battle. Remember when you were a little kid and you would get in trouble in school? Your parents would meet with the teacher and talk to them on your behalf, intercede for you. We do the same thing with Saint Michael, we ask him to plead with God on our behalf. Wouldn't you want the most powerful angel pleading with God on your behalf? Think of Aragorn in *Lord of the Rings*. Think of Captain James T. Kirk in *Star Trek*. Think of Achilles in the battle of Troy. Think of the greatest warriors in all of the greatest warrior movies, books, and legends and roll them into one and you might get somewhere close to the strength of Saint Michael. Just think, that strength is defending *you* in battle. The great captains and commanders ready themselves for war with battle cries, armor and strength, and we must ready ourselves for battle and this prayer is an incredible place to start. The strength of Saint Michael, great warrior of heaven, is your protection against all the wickedness and sinister plots of the devil. Then, join that power with the power of God and thrust Satan back into hell. Some translations of this prayer ask that God and Saint Michael would cast Satan back into hell. The word thrust sounds so much more forceful. Don't just slap him on the wrist and tell him to go home, kick him out of our hearts and send him packing for good. What a knockout punch! This prayer is short, and yet it is full of courage and words to fight. It can and does fill us with strength as we begin to feel Saint Michael defending us and the power of God mounting and growing beside us in this battle for our souls.

Sometimes in this battle we need a more centering prayer, perhaps one that is less focused on the clamor and clashing of the battle at hand, but instead draws us closer to the very heart of God. In such a need, Saint John Vianney shares one of his personal prayers with us,

> "I love you, O my God, and my only desire is to love you until the last breath of my life. I love you, O my infinitely lovable God, and I would rather die loving you, than live without loving you. I love you, Lord, and the only grace I ask is to love you eternally. . . My God, if my tongue cannot say in every moment that I love you, I want my heart to repeat it to you as often as I draw breath."[17]

This prayer may not pack the battle-cry punch that the Saint Michael the Archangel prayer does, but it is just as powerful. Sometimes when I feel weak I don't want to pray a prayer to enter into battle, in fact, I'd rather hide from the battle altogether. In those moments I find that this prayer is a great help as it focuses on my love of God more than anything else. The words of Saint John Vianney speak to my heart as he prays that his love for God may be repeated by his heart in every moment of every day. What beautiful words and what a wondrous challenge to live out. Such a deepening of my love for God can only bring about more love, strength, and readiness for the battle at hand.

---

[17] CCC 2658

If you are in the neighborhood for a little longer prayer that packs an unmistakable punch to Satan, look no further than the prayers of Saint John Chrysostom. Chrysostom means "golden tongue" and he is named so because his words had and have a way of getting people to rise up and be inspired to live for the Lord. His prayers are among those commonly used in exorcisms to cast out demons. The strength and vigor of these prayers is impossible to miss or mistake for anything short of the awesome power of God. Chrysostom prays,

> "Satan: The Lord rebukes thee by His frightful name! Shudder, tremble, be afraid, depart, be utterly destroyed, be banished! [You] who fell from heaven and together with [you] all evil spirits: every evil spirit of lust, the spirit of evil...or one altering the mind of man. Depart swiftly from this creature of the Creator Christ our God! And be gone from the servant/handmaid of God, from his/her mind, from his/her soul, from his/her heart, from his/her reins, from his/her senses, from all his/her members, that he/she might become whole and sound and free, knowing God, his/her own Master and Creator of all things."[18]

What power! And to think, that is only *part* of the prayer! This section of the prayer starts with a punch, by telling Satan to be afraid. We remind Satan that the Lord rebukes him and that the name of the Lord alone is powerful beyond measure and incites

---

[18] Chrysostom, Saint John. "Exorcism." *OrthodoxWiki*. Web. 22 May 2012. <http://orthodoxwiki.org/Exorcism>.

fear in Satan. Satan's fear is deeper though, for it is not just enough that he is afraid of the name of the Lord. Satan should shudder and tremble, be utterly and completely destroyed and banished all by the name of the Lord. I

so often find that I need to be reminded of the power of His Name. God is mighty and powerful on His own to be sure, but it is so important to take a step back and realize just how powerful His Name is all on its own. Not just Satan himself, but all the evil spirits who accompany Satan and do his bidding, are banished by the power of the name of the Lord. This prayer reminds us that we are creatures, reflections, beautiful images of the Creator and in so reminding us of this truth we are reminded that we are made for Him and Him alone. Finally, we, together with the power of God, send Satan packing from our heads, our souls, our hearts, our minds, our senses, and everything about us. We let him know that he is not welcome in or around us. Period. May we all be whole and sound and free, knowing God and strengthened by Him for all of our days. By our example of vulnerability and openness, may we be strengthened for the battle at hand, standing firm in God's love and in the life-changing truth that He finds us worthy.

Dignity

"We all have veiled our glory, or someone has veiled it for us. Usually, some combination of both. But, the time has come to set all veils aside." – John Eldredge[1]

The painful truth is that we have veiled our glory. We've all done it; no one escapes this charge by simply pleading innocent. We've veiled our God-given glory with lies, doubt, insecurities, and fear. We've allowed our glory to be veiled by the Father of Lies. We've let him into our hearts and as we've been locked away in coffin after coffin, and we've also let our glory and our dignity be veiled, until the veils became so thick that we forgot there was even a bright and radiant glory underneath it all. The time has come to set the veils aside, to rip them off because they cover up and hide the beauty and wonder that God created in each of us. Just as a lamp is not to be hidden under a bushel basket, and a city on a hill cannot be hidden, our glory and our dignity as women was not created to be hidden or shoved away. The reality is that our world is desperately in need of women who know that they are worthy, not because they deem themselves to be so, but because God deems them so. Such a woman lights up the room, challenges women and men to become better versions of themselves and change the world for the better. We are needed and we can no longer hide the glory and dignity that God created us with beneath veils. The time has come; let us allow God to shine through us.

---

[1] Eldredge, John. *Waking the Dead: The Glory of a Heart Fully Alive.* Nashville, TN: Thomas Nelson, 2003. 74.

What It Means

We all get lost from time to time. We forget that we are worthy; we forget that there is a God who loves us more passionately than we could ever imagine. We fail to remember that, no matter how many times we fall and sin, His love for us remains as true as it ever was. We forget that His love is constant, unfailing, unchanging, unwavering, timeless, eternal, and steadfast. We also forget that the lost get found. Read the parables in the Gospels and you will see that not only do the lost get found, but God rejoices perhaps even more over the lost being found than anything else. The Prodigal Son. The Lost Coin. The Lost Sheep. Each tale is a metaphor for the joy that God has when someone who is lost is found in Him. We are found by love and by grace, by nothing short of the miracle of His love. The journey of being lost is an easy one; we've done it countless times in our lives. The journey to being found, and, more importantly, being found by Him is much more difficult. We try to be found by so many other things, by guys in bars, our parents, our friends, our bosses, and our significant others. But we will never be truly found by them until we are first found, wholly and completely, by God. Being found in Him may be more difficult, but because it is so much more difficult, it is all the more beautiful, and all the more worth the struggle.

An ideal wife, a woman worthy of praise, is clothed, she is strong, and she has dignity. Most people hear the word dignity and think they know what it means, but actually defining it proves to be a much more difficult concept. Dignity is one of those words we know in context but struggle to define exactly what it means, what it looks like, and how we can espouse such a virtue. The definition of dignity makes my heart sing:

1. Bearing, conduct, or speech indicative of self-respect or appreciation of the formality or gravity of an occasion or situation.
2. Nobility or elevation of character; worthiness.
3. Elevated rank.[2]

The first definition sounds a bit wordy to me, but I latch on to "self-respect". A woman who is worthy respects herself because she knows she is a creation of God, and a daughter of the Most High. A woman of worth will be clothed, and a woman who is clothed will have more self-confidence – though not always instantaneously – and therefore be a stronger woman. She will also have an appreciation for each situation that life puts her in, and because of her modesty and strength, she will know how to act accordingly. Call it the trickle-down effect if you will, a woman who respects herself is more likely to be more confident, and therefore not need to dress scantily, and will also be stronger in the way she carries herself, and in the way that she opens her heart to God. Self-respect is a wonderful trait for any woman to have, and a necessary quality for a woman of worth to have, but dignity doesn't end there.

The second definition simply and beautifully says what I struggle to put into words. Nobility. What woman doesn't want to be noble? Aren't we all princesses at heart? Certainly! We are

---

[2] "Dignity." *Dictionary.com*. Dictionary.com. Web. <http://dictionary.reference.com/browse/dignity?s=t>.

daughters of the King, so not only are we princesses at heart, but we are also princesses of the Kingdom of Heaven. We were made for nobility. We may not all want the fame and the paperwork that goes with being a princess, but the honor and the glory due to such a woman, that is something we all long for. What we fail to realize, however, is that by the merits of grace, we are already princesses. We need to be reminded, and constantly, that what our heart desires – nobility, beauty, honor, and dignity – are already ours. We are daughters of the King of Kings, and the daughter of a king is what? A princess. So what is a daughter of the King of Kings? The Princess of Princesses. The cream of the crop. If the King of Kings is the king to end all kings, the great ruler of all creation, doesn't it follow that we, as His daughters, are called to the best of the best, the greatest princesses, the ones with *the most* elevated character? We are the princesses to end all princesses, the noblest of the nobles, and the worthiest of all the ladies in the land.

Where does this elevated character (read: dignity) come from? Let's go back to the trickle-down effect. The elevated character comes from knowing the Truth in our hearts; it comes from knowing Jesus and allowing Him to fill us with His love. God lays the foundation in our hearts, and by turning to Him, we build on this foundation together. We build self-respect, modesty, strength, hope, faith, love, all of these go into the foundation and make it stronger as we add friends, family, relationships, community, and fellowship. Our elevated character comes from the knowledge and belief that we are daughters of God. Such a belief must come from deep within our souls, and it must rest upon the foundation that God builds in our hearts. The reality that we are daughters of God is not something that can simply be thrown out with the bath water; it elevates our rank in a way that is both humbling and uplifting. It gives us a grace and a peace about us that flows from within – it makes our souls shine and our faces light up. We seem to walk on the clouds. A woman who has dignity that comes from within glides, floats, and radiates His love. We have dignity because we are forgiven. Rather than being constantly weighed down by our sins, we seek the loving forgiveness of the Father, and are restored to communion with Him.

Then, at long last, comes part two of the second definition: worthiness! My God, You wash us in Your love! How perfect that the very word this entire book is based on is in the definition of what it means to have dignity. How serendipitous! God is constantly reminding us that we are worthy. It all comes back to being worthy. The world tells us we are not worthy, that there is no way we could be worthy, but the Scriptures, the Saints, Tradition, the Sacraments, the Church, and Jesus Himself tell us over and over again that we are. We need to hear it and we keep coming back to it – or perhaps it keeps coming back to us – because we don't get it yet. We let the world take over and we forget that we are worthy. The ideal wife, the woman worthy of praise, and every single daughter and son of God is clothed in worthiness. She doesn't just know that she is worthy in her soul, she is clothed in it. She wraps herself in her worthiness, she covers herself with it, and her worthiness keeps her warm. Her worthiness is all about her, and all around her – it never leaves her.

Imperfect and Yet Dignified

Let's face it: we are imperfect beings. We falter, stumble, trip, and fall more often than we'd ever care to admit. At times it seems that there is nothing we are more aware of than our shortcomings. In light of our faults, and fully aware of them, how are we to maintain our dignity? The simple truth is that we aren't the ones who maintain our own dignity, God is. The dignity we possess, just like our worthiness, is not ours based on our own merit. Rather, it is a gift, freely and unconditionally given to us by the loving Father who created us. Our dignity, and our worthiness, comes from God, who is eternally dignified and perpetually worthy of all the praise and honor our hearts can offer.

We often hear people say that they can't wait to get to Heaven in hopes of hearing God tell them, "well done, good and faithful servant." It took me a long time to realize exactly what *isn't* in that phrase: perfection. We will not arrive at Heaven and hear God say "well done, good and perfect servant." We are imperfect beings, but what He is looking for is the faithful servant. Though we falter and fail, He isn't looking for perfection: perfection resides in Him. He is looking for the servant that, even though they get lost, always tries to find their way home, back into His heart. We have dignity, not on our own merit or deeds, but because we are reflections of the perfect God who created us, and the perfect God we are striving to imitate. We have dignity by His loving and merciful grace. God's dignity and glory remain God's dignity and glory despite our shortcomings. The only question God asks of us is, "Will you keep trying? For love of Me? I promise I will be by your side." Tenth Avenue North, in their song, "By Your Side," tells us that God will be by our side always, whether it is the dead of night, or the light of day. The band invites us to remember that God's hands our holding us so we shouldn't fight them because God wants to stay by our side. His hands hold you no matter where you fall, no matter how deep the darkness you've fallen into is He still holds you. He longs to call you the faithful servant, will you answer?

Often times we feel that purity and dignity are interrelated. While they are distinct characteristics, they are often connected, especially when we talk about a woman of worth. Perhaps you haven't been as pure in your life as you or God would have hoped. The struggles of purity and chastity are real, and the wounds they leave us with are deep and shameful. More often than not people think that a woman who has dignity must also be pure, and that a woman who has lost her purity to any degree can no longer be a woman of dignity. This is yet another lie of the devil. Blessed Pope John Paul II talked a great deal about purity and he often said that there are two types of purity: purity of body and purity of heart and mind. One, once lost, can never be fully regained. This is a wound that only Christ Himself can heal. However, we are not without hope. Our purity of heart and mind can be restored, fully and completely. Our dignity is not lost. We make the choice to restore our purity of heart and mind by choosing to rid ourselves of temptation. If we choose to enter into relationships, we set boundaries and enter relationships carefully, and avoid the near occasions of sin. We frequent confession so that we can always remain close to His heart, and so that His grace may wash over us, strengthening us in the battle for purity. We do our best to rid ourselves of friends, situations, and circumstances that threaten our purity. There is no hard and fast rule here; what threatens my purity may not be a threat at all to your purity. But rest assured there is hope that our dignity is not lost just because we have struggled with purity in our lives. Don't let Satan sell you on yet another lie that threatens your worthiness. No matter where you've been, what you've done, or how far from grace you feel you've fallen, your purity of heart and mind can be restored. Your glory and dignity need not be veiled forever. Choose to let God restore you to purity, and so restore you to the dignity with which He created you.

Perfect Dignity

Whenever I'm struggling with something, I find comfort in finding an example that parallels my struggles. It is reassuring to know that I am not alone in my struggles, and it also gives me hope that my struggles can be conquered. Who better to look to than Mary when we are struggling? Her dignity is perfect, untouched, and untainted by sin. No matter how much people looked down on her or judged her for being pregnant before the appropriate time, God maintained and restored her dignity.

Some might think that our struggles don't at all parallel Mary's. After all, she was assumed into Heaven as a virgin so she never really struggled with purity, right? I would think that when Mary arrived in Heaven, God could have actually said to her, "Well done, good and perfect servant" because she was without sin. She didn't know what it is like to mess up, to fool around with a guy, or push those lines of purity just a little too far. She doesn't know what it is like to find out that you have a sexually transmitted disease from some guy you may never see again. Perhaps Mary never knew those temptations, but that doesn't mean she can't relate or that we can't find hope in her.

Often times I don't think Mary would have thought of herself as a particularly dignified woman. She had dignity to be sure, but when I think of Mary, I think first of her humility, and second of the dignity that God gave her. She knew in her heart that her purity was intact and that her innocence had never been lost. Just because she knew that truth doesn't mean that everyone else believed the same to be true. The movie *The Nativity Story* does a beautiful job of showing Mary's humble dignity. She returns to Nazareth after having been with her cousin Elizabeth and it is discovered that she is with child. For such a crime she could have been stoned to death, and Joseph, her betrothed, would have been the first to cast a stone. In the scene when she first returns to Nazareth, Joseph simply stares in disbelief as one of Mary's siblings rubs her growing baby bump. Mary's siblings look on in wonder, awe, and joy. Joseph stares, awe struck, though clearly not in the same way Mary's siblings are. Mary, filled with trust in God's plan, departs from the cart and returns to her home. She doesn't run and hide in shame, she holds herself with dignity, because no matter what others may think, she knows the truth. She may not know God's plan in its entirety, but she trusts that God has asked her to take part in it for some special purpose. She also knows that Truth itself has made its dwelling in her womb. Mary never sinned but that doesn't mean she didn't experience trials or the whispers and rumors of those around her. Despite it all, God maintained her dignity and gave Joseph the courage to take Mary in as his wife, and so provided shelter for her from the gossip and the unjust glances of those around them. Her strength and dignity remained intact because her dependence on God was so unwavering.

Our struggles in life may be radically different from what Mary struggled with, and yet in many ways they are the same struggles. We face gossip, unkind looks from strangers, other people are sure they know what we've done and who we've done what with. Countless people will have theories about who we are, what we've done, and how we've fallen short. But we find hope in Mary because through the trials of her life, from the conception of Jesus to His death on Calvary, and her own assumption into Heaven, she endured, and God Himself maintained and restored her dignity. She shows us the perfect example of firm dependence on God and what that can mean for our lives: peace through the trials of life, unshaken dignity, humility, and, for Mary, the being crowned the Queen of Heaven. If we come to depend on God the way that Mary did then we will find our dignity maintained, our good name restored, and someday we shall join Mary in Heaven.

Renewed, Refreshed, Restored

Crystalina Evert is a beautiful modern day woman whose dignity has been restored. In high school she lost her virginity and went through a number of impure relationships until, at long last, she encountered Truth and gave up her old lifestyle in favor of a life lived for God. When Crystalina gives her testimony she says a number of times, "It doesn't matter who you are, where you've been, what you've done, or what kind of brokenness you have, God is bigger than all of it."[3] I've heard her testimony often and this phrase of hers never changes because it is a message we need to hear over and over because we forget it far too easily. I find myself waiting for this phrase in her testimony because it fills me with hope and confidence that our purity, our honor, and our worthiness can be restored.

We somehow think that we will be the exception to God's unconditional love. We think that unlike anyone before us, we have gone too far, sinned too much, or are too broken for God to heal. When we believe that we are the exception to God's immeasurable love, we sell His love and our worth short. We buy into another one of Satan's lies. There is no place that God can't go. There is no valley so deep that God's love cannot penetrate it. There is no darkness so profound that God's light cannot illuminate it. There is no brokenness so tragic and so shattered that God's merciful love cannot heal it. Our God is the God of second chances. John reminds us in the book of Revelations that God can and does "make all things new."[4]

God never leaves us. He renews us, He refreshes us, and He restores us. Switchfoot sings of this beautiful truth in their song "Always", singing that, though there are scars deep in our hearts, God is always ours. The band begins to sing hallelujah as we cave in and let God into our hearts, knowing that every breath is a second chance to live in His love. These scars are indeed deep in our heart, we have been born into this place that seems so desolate, so hopeless, and yet despite it all, He is always ours.

---

[3] "Crystalina's Testimony." Interview by Women Made New. *Women Made New.* <womenmadenew.com>.

[4] Revelation 21:5.

Hallelujah, we are caving in; we are letting Him in our hearts. Praise God – which is the literal translation of Hallelujah – every breath is a second chance. He makes all things new. Every moment is a second chance to be renewed, refreshed, and restored to hope, dignity, and His love reigning in our hearts.

No matter who you are, where you've been, what you've done, or how far you think you've fallen from grace, Jesus invites you to find yourself beside His still waters. They bring about peace and hope. We can still hold our heads high. We can walk tall in the knowledge that, no matter what the world thinks of us, His love for us remains. Beside His still waters we are refreshed and filled with His love. Resting near His waters we are reminded that God will remain constant and true, restoring us to hope, beauty, dignity, and ultimately, worthiness.

Laughter

"Be kind, for everyone you know is facing a great battle"
— Philo of Alexandria

Some days I just don't feel like laughing. Some days I roll out of bed and get out on the wrong side and I just don't have any laughter in me. What is there to laugh at? We all have those days. We wake up late, the coffee pot stops working the same day our blow dryer finally gives out and our mascara clumps beyond use. Sure, we could laugh at all of those mishaps, but that laughter isn't a laughter of joy, it is a laughter at how annoying life can get. If we weren't laughing we'd probably be crying; sometimes one leads to the other. So what on God's green earth does the author of Proverbs 31 mean in saying that the ideal wife "laughs at the days to come"? What are we laughing at in the days to come? More of the same crazy antics of life? Are we supposed to keep laughing this fake, often bitter laugh at the days to come? I hardly think that is what Scripture could be referring to. For that matter, what are we laughing at today? God has a great and brilliant sense of humor, I am sure of it. However, I don't always share His same divine sense of humor.

What are we laughing at today? Take a moment and really think about what you've laughed about today. Yesterday. This week. What have you really and truly laughed at with an honest, joyful laugh? God knows I've spent time laughing at the ridiculousness of life. I jokingly laugh at the traffic jam on the freeway, at the fact that I left my lunch on the kitchen counter at home, and at my toe that I stubbed for the third time this week. But what have I joyfully laughed at? I admit that this list is much harder to recall, which is perhaps all the more reason to hold on to it. I've laughed at the beauty of God in the mountains. I've laughed at small children behind me in the movie theatre shouting, "OH, that must have *hurt!*" in their beautifully innocent way. I've chuckled at the jokes my mother makes about changing the locks on the house to keep me from eating all of her food when I come for a visit. I've laughed at myself while, when on a beautiful hike I tried to climb over a downed tree in my path, only to have the branches break underneath me, leaving me to fall backwards into a giant pile of snow. Proverbs 31:25 tells us that not only are the ideal wife and the woman of worth clothed, with strength and dignity no less, but that she laughs at the days to come. In order to laugh at the days to come, we have to learn to laugh with joy at the present days.

Finding Peace

A good friend of mine once told me that if we work too hard for what lies ahead of us we will never to know what it is like to experience the joy of the present moment. If we focus so intensely on trying to laugh at the days to come, we risk forgetting to laugh at the times, the joy, and the beauty of the life that is right in front of us.

So how do we laugh at the times before us? Some days, most days even, it seems too difficult to fathom laughing at what lies before us. What lies before us is a giant stack of laundry, bills that need to be paid, a job that brings stress to our lives, and relationships that are falling apart at the seams. We can come up with a never ending list of things *not* to laugh at. It is in these moments when we tally up all of our woes that we fall back on the strength of God, and we ask Him to reveal to us the joy and laughter in our lives. We start by finding peace, and by acknowledging that there are certain things in our lives that we will never fully have control over. Once we accept that we are not, nor will we ever be fully in control (and thank God for that, quite literally) we can enter into His peace and trust Him more fully. Trusting that He will take care of us we can begin to see the humor in life. Reliant on His plan for our lives we learn to chuckle at His ironic timing. We can laugh at the ridiculousness of life because we know and trust that He is in control.

Ecclesiastes speaks quite eloquently about the beauty and timing of life. The author writes, "There is an appointed time for everything, and a time for every affair under the heavens…a time to weep, and a time to laugh; a time to mourn, and a time to dance."[5] There are times to laugh and there are times to cry. Simply because Proverbs 31:25 says that the woman of worth laughs at the days to come doesn't mean that she is constantly laughing. Everything will happen according to His plan. Ecclesiastes continues, "He has made everything appropriate to its time, and has put the timeless into their hearts, without men's ever discovering, from beginning to end, the work which God has done."[6] God has put every single thing, from the minutest detail to our biggest life decisions, to its appropriate time. He has even put the timeless – Himself – in our hearts without us ever knowing. It is not as though we wake up from some surgery one morning and discover Him in our hearts, He has always been there. God has

---

[5] Ecclesiastes 3:1, 4.

[6] Ecclesiastes 3:11.

always been at work in our lives, even if we haven't always realized it. The author of Ecclesiastes concludes, "I recognized that there is nothing better than to be glad and to do well during life...I recognized that whatever God does will endure forever; there is no adding to it, or taking from it. Thus has God done that he may be revered. What now is has already been; what is to be, already is; and God restores what would otherwise be displaced."[7] Trusting in God's perfect plan for our lives, even when it seems imperfect to us, we too come to recognize that there is nothing better than to be glad and do well in life. Certainly there are times that we will have struggles and we will suffer, but the suffering passes, and we return to His love for us, trusting that we can, despite the heart break, be glad in life. We know that whatever God does will endure forever because His love is already enduring and lasting throughout eternity. His love is unfading. We cannot add to, nor take from, His perfect plan. What exists now has already existed, what is to come has already come, because God is outside of time. He restores us, even if we find ourselves displaced. God sees us, seeks us, pursues us, and finds us worthy. He rests our hearts in His continual promise of eternal love and fills us with His peace so that we can begin to laugh at the present days.

When we, as women of worth, speak of laughing at the days before us, we speak of laughing in a charitable sense of the word. We aren't laughing at others, at their struggles, or at their joys in order to make ourselves feel better. As Jesus tells us in Luke's gospel account, "Be merciful, just as [also] your Father is

---

[7] Ecclesiastes 3:12, 14-15.

merciful."[8] Be kind to others because you never know what they are facing. Perhaps they lost their job, their spouse, their child, or all of the above. Perhaps they are a modern day Job. Everyone is facing a great battle, a cross that Christ has asked them to carry, and laughing at others is certainly not what the author of Proverbs was referring to. When we judge or compare ourselves to others, we have no hope of joyful laughing at the present time or for filling our hearts with peace. When you judge someone, you do not define them, you define yourself. When we compare ourselves with others we will always find a way to fall short. We define ourselves as imperfect because we lack what someone else has. If we compare ourselves to our best friends we fall short because they own a house, have a loving husband, and seem to have life all figured out. If we compare ourselves to our co-worker we fall short because she works more hours and makes more money than we do. If we compare ourselves to our own mothers we fall short because she is happily married to the man of her dreams. No matter who we compare ourselves to we can always find at least one way that we fall short. By comparing ourselves to others we begin to chip away at the peace that God places in our hearts, and the ability to laugh at the life He has placed before us becomes a nearly impossible task. Blessed Mother Teresa said "If you judge people, you have no time to love them." Comparing ourselves to others and judging them for having something that we lack precludes us from loving them as we ought to. Jesus goes on to say, "But to you who hear I say, love your enemies, do good to those who hate you, bless those who curse you, pray for those

---

[8] Luke 6:36.

who mistreat you."[9] By loving others, whether they persecute, mistreat us, or not, we open our hearts to God's love and allow His unconditional love to flow through us. Such openness to His love only brings about good in our lives, and creates ripples of love to others. Jesus continues, "For if you love those who love you, what credit is that to you? Even sinners love those who love them."[10] When we love everyone and stop comparing ourselves to others, we open our hearts to love and to God's peace.

By keeping our hearts from judging others and comparing ourselves to them, we follow the advice of the psalmist who writes, "Happy those who do not follow the counsel of the wicked, nor go the way of sinners, nor sit in company with scoffers. Rather, the law of the Lord is their joy."[11] The law of the Lord is our joy, and we find peace by following the One who is without sin, and who is not only filled with love but is Love personified. We heed the advice of the psalmist and we find that we are happy because we aren't following the counsel of the wicked who pushes us and drives us to compare ourselves with others. Instead, we are filled with joy with Him, who is Love incarnate.

The Days to Come

Looking out at our future – is it scary? Hopeful? Joyful? A dark bottomless pit? The footnotes on Proverbs 31:25 tell us that to laugh at the days to come means that a woman of worth "anticipates the future with gladness free from anxiety."[12] We are

---

[9] Luke 6:27.

[10] Luke 6:32.

[11] Psalm 1:1-2.

[12] Footnote on Proverbs 31:25, NAB.

to be unafraid of the future, trusting completely in God's plan for our lives. Surely we know that this is far easier said than done. So where do we start? We started by finding peace in the present moment and giving everything to God. Clay Walker sings in his song "Fall" that we can always fall, we can fall apart into God's arms, knowing that He will catch us every time. He invites us to lose it all, every single doubt and fear, every worry, and every tear, because God is right here, waiting for us to fall into His arms.

Resting in His peace we can look to the future. We see that God has taken care of us all of our lives. Aware that He has always taken care of us, and is continuing to take care of us, we begin to let go of the anxieties we have about our future. It may be scary, it may be unknown, but we trust that He will continue to guide us. Our plans for our lives, for love, our careers, and our families may change and we may begin to think that our future is a bottomless pit. We may begin to be filled with anxiety at the fact that some or all of our plans have changed. Still, we are invited to hold fast to His love for us. Holding fast to His love, resting in the palm of His hands, we can begin to anticipate our futures with gladness, freed from anxiety.

Sure, we can find ourselves relaxing peacefully in God's hands. We can even begin to anticipate the future free from anxiety, but doesn't this verse in Proverbs call us to more? The ideal wife isn't simply supposed to anticipate her future free from anxiety, she is supposed to be so freed from anxiety that she laughs at her future. A woman of worth doesn't just laugh at anything, much less anyone. She laughs "at the days to come." When I first read that I thought, "What does that mean?" She laughs at the future? I can't imagine kindly, honestly, or joyfully laughing at the future. Whenever I laugh about my future it is more to cover up my pain, in much the same way that I often find myself laughing at the days before me. Thinking about my future I find myself laughing, knowing that I may never make much money in this life. I laugh realizing that I was not married by the time I was 23, even though it was something I dreamt about for a long time. I laugh because the days to come aren't what I thought they were going to be, nor are the days of the past. Then, praised be Jesus, I noticed the footnote on this verse. I literally laughed out loud at this footnote. I surely anticipate the future with joy, I dream about it a lot, but it is hardly ever free of anxiety. In fact, more often than not when I anticipate the future I am *filled* with anxiety. I wonder how I'm ever going to make ends meet. I wonder that if I can't make ends meet, will it ever be possible to save up, or pay off my loans and actually enjoy life? I wonder how I could ever pay for even the simplest of weddings. I wonder if I will ever meet the man I am supposed to marry, or if I've already met him and he's walked away, or I've walked away. I wonder if he'll ever really want to commit to marrying me with all of my crazy quirks. If, by the grace of God we do meet, fall in love, and get married, how are we ever going to afford to have kids? A house? Will I be happy as a mother or will I hate it? The questions go on and on and the anxiety increases. But that, dear friends, is not what a woman of worth or the "Ideal Wife" is made of. She, by some miracle of heaven, is free of anxiety.

How does anyone, *especially* a woman, get to be free of anxiety? In the Second Roman Missal, when we prayed the Our

Father, the priest would say this prayer, "deliver us, Lord, from every evil, and grant us peace in our day. In Your mercy keep us free from sin and protect us from all anxiety as we wait in joyful hope for the coming of our Savior, Jesus Christ."[13] After all this thought, contemplation and analysis I kept coming back to one question: *How?* How are we supposed to magically, divinely, be freed from anxiety? The answer is simple and lies before us: prayer. It is no mistake that while we are praying the Our Father at the Lord's Supper, the only prayer Jesus taught His apostles and disciples, the priest prays that we would be freed from anxiety. Through prayer we slowly rid ourselves of ourselves and fill ourselves with God. In the Third Roman Missal the priest prays, "By the help of Your mercy, we may always be free from sin and safe from all distress."[14] The words may have changed but the meaning is the same. When we enter into prayer we are freed from anxiety and kept safe from all distress. By freeing ourselves, or rather, by allowing God to free us from anxiety and distress, we are no longer weighed down by worry and can joyfully laugh with eager hope at whatever He has planned for us. We trust the words that prophet Jeremiah tells us, that God's plans for us are "for [our] welfare, not for woe! Plans to give you a future full of hope."[15] His plans are only for things that we can handle with Him by our side. We may not be able to handle things or life situations on our own, but rest assured, He will be with us, strengthening us to handle

---

[13] "USCCB - Roman Missal | Priest Changes - Communion Rite." *USCCB - Roman Missal | Priest Changes - Communion Rite*. United States Conference of Catholic Bishops. Web. <http://old.usccb.org/romanmissal/samples-priest-communion.shtml>.

[14] Ibid.

[15] Jeremiah 29:11.

whatever life throws at us. He reminds us, "When you call me, when you go to pray to me, I will listen to you. When you look for me, you will find me. Yes, when you seek me with all your heart, you will find me with you."[16] When we seek Him with all of our heart we find that He has already been with us and has remained with us. If you want to be freed from anxiety so that you can laugh at the days to come, seek the Lord with all of your heart.

The Beauty of Surrender

The answer to being freed from anxiety is not to fight harder, but to surrender. Sometimes we need to fight the good fight and battle against anxiety. Fighting the good fight is often necessary, especially when we are fighting Satan. But other times in life we need to surrender. There is a special grace to discerning the difference in what our call to action is. Through continued prayer God will reveal to us whether we are called to fight or surrender. Saint John tells us in one of his letters,

> "Beloved, do not trust every spirit but test the spirits to see whether they belong to God, because many false prophets have gone out into the word. This is how you can know the Spirit of God: every spirit that acknowledges Jesus Christ come in the flesh belongs to God, and every spirit that does not acknowledge Jesus does not belong to God."[17]

---

[16] Jeremiah 29:12-14.
[17] 1 John 4:1-3a.

Pray about your own heart and anxieties, are your worries acknowledging Jesus Christ, or are your worries about things that you cannot control, and therefore need to relinquish to Jesus? Saint John continues, "You belong to God, children, and you have conquered them, for the one who is in you is greater than the one who is in the world. They belong to the world; accordingly their teaching belongs to the world, and the world listens to them...This is how we know the spirit of truth and the spirit of deceit."[18] God lives in your heart, and He is greater than Satan. Who are you listening to: the world or God? Rest your fears in Him.

PRAY

Who are we surrendering to, and why do we need to surrender? We are surrendering to God. We hold up our white flags and admit that we get worried, stressed, and anxious. We need to surrender because we can't bear this load of life on our own. We surrender through prayer.

Pause
Reflect
Ask
Yield

In life it is so easy to get caught up in the myriad of things we want or need to get done. We get busy and we feel like we are running a million miles a minute, or at least our brains are running that fast, and we wish our bodies could keep up the pace. We need to

---

[18] 1 John 4:4-5, 6b

pause. We need to stop holding down the fast forward button as though our lives depended on it. We simply pause – we don't stop the movie forever, but we pause – we take a breath and focus on God. By pausing we allow ourselves a moment to slow down and to focus on what and who is truly important. We can take a deep breath and thank God for the blessings of our day. Take a minute and simply pause. Rest your heart in God. Pause and find yourself in His hands. Allow Him to hold you in His loving arms.

Next, reflect. Reflect on what is causing you to be so stressed and anxious. All too often I find that I get so stressed and the littlest things can set me off. When I take a moment to pause and reflect, I find that I don't really know what it is I'm stressing about. The tension mounts but when I take a step back, I find that in reality there really isn't that much that should be stressing me out. That isn't always the case, but even when there are legitimate reasons to be stressed, taking a second or two to reflect helps me recognize what is causing the tension and worry in my life.

Aware of what is creating the stress and worry, we can now ask God for guidance. We pause and reflect so that we can know what to ask God for. When we reflect we can pinpoint areas we are struggling and then take those areas and struggles to God. Perhaps it is your children running around coloring on the walls. *"God, help me to be patient with my children. Fill me with Your unconditional love."* Maybe it is your significant other who is stressed out themselves and adding to your own anxiety. *"Precious Lord, thank You for bringing this love into my life, please ease their stress. Hold their heart. Reveal to them Your love and fill them with trust for You. May easing their stress ease mine as well."* It could even be that after pausing and reflecting you are unsure what is causing an increase in stress. *"Father in Heaven, my heart is lost and confused. I am filled with stress and anxiety and I feel so buried in it that I can't find the cause. Help me to keep my head above water. Open my eyes to what is making my heart uneasy, walk me through it, and let Your love reduce and eliminate the tension."* Scripture tells us over and over again that if we seek the Lord He will come, and that whatever we ask in Jesus' name will be granted. Saint Teresa of Avila said, "You pay God a compliment by asking great things of Him." Be not afraid to ask big things of our big God.

Finally, yield. Surrender. Ask for big things of God and then leave your requests in His hands. Know that you have made your worries and fears known to God and that it is pointless to worry anymore. As Saint Paul wrote to the church in Philippi, "Have no anxiety at all, but in everything, by prayer and petition, make your requests known to God. Then the peace of God that surpasses all understanding will guard your hearts and minds in Christ Jesus."[19] Have no more anxiety. Instead, make your petitions and worries, stresses and uneasiness known to God in prayer, and then allow Jesus to surround your heart and free it from worry. His peace is beyond all our understanding. The fact that His peace is beyond understanding makes it mysterious, intriguing, and inviting. Jesus speaks to us saying, "Therefore I tell you, do not worry about your life, what you will eat [or drink], or

---

[19] Philippians 4:6-7.

about your body, what you will wear."[20] Jesus doesn't want us to worry. He tells us that the birds do not gather or collect anything and yet the Father takes care of them, why would He not also take care of us? Jesus asks, "Can any of your by worrying add a single moment to your life-span? Why are you anxious?"[21] Take a moment to pause, breathe, and get some perspective on just how much the Father takes care of you. Jesus goes on to tell us, "All these things [food, drink, clothing] the pagans seek. Your heavenly Father knows that you need them all. But seek first the kingdom [of God] and his righteousness, and all these things will be given you besides. Do not worry about tomorrow; tomorrow will take care of itself. Sufficient for a day is its own evil."[22] I can just imagine God sitting on His heavenly throne looking down with fatherly amusement at His children, "Stop worrying. I've got this. Let me handle it, today, tomorrow, and every day after that. Let me love you." Learn to pray; pause, reflect, ask, and yield, and you will find peace and freedom from anxiety, and you will be able to laugh with joy and eager anticipation at the days to come. Let Him shower you in His love and peace.

The beauty of surrender is that by dying to ourselves, to our own worries and fears, we can begin to rise to His plan for our lives. The dying and the letting go is a painful process, but it must and needs to be done. Jesus didn't want to be scourged and spat upon. I'm sure He didn't wake up one morning and say to His Father, "Gee, I feel like being whipped and beaten, spit upon and

---

[20] Matthew 6:25.

[21] Matthew 6:27-28.

[22] Matthew 6:32-34.

mocked today. Doesn't that sound like fun? Can You arrange that for me?" Of course He follows His Father's will, but the process was not an easy one. In the Garden of Gethsemane Christ prayed that the cup would pass from Him, but ultimately that if it would not, if He had to die, Jesus prayed that the Father's will would be accomplished. We unite the suffering we feel when we struggle with Christ's sufferings. Christ had to die so that He could rise and triumph over sin and death. So too we must surrender our worries and anxieties to Him so that we can rise to His perfect plan for our lives. There is a poem called "Broken Dreams" by an unknown author that gets at the heart of our struggle to surrender:

As children bring their broken toys
with tears for us to mend,
I brought my broken dreams to God
because He was my friend.

But then instead of leaving Him
in peace to work alone,
I hung around and tried to help
with ways that were my own.

At last I snatched them back
and cried,
"How can You be so slow?"
"My child," He said,
"What could I do?
You never did let go."

We have to let go if He is ever going to fix our brokenness. We have to let Him fix us in His own way and in His time if we are ever going to reach a point where we can laugh at the days to come. Surrendering is not easy but it is necessary. Thank goodness Christ has already shown us the way.

Another beautiful aspect of surrender is that by laying down our own lives, our beauty shines all the more as we become more dependent on the One who never fails. Our beauty shines because when we surrender we are emptied of ourselves and filled with God, and God's beauty radiates in our hearts. As Matt Maher sings in his song, "Letting Go", there is a beauty and a grace when we can say to God that we are holding onto His love and letting go of ourselves. There is a grace when we can say so long to everything else because we just want to be in God's arms, moving closer to His heart. We let go of our anxiety, of our worry, and we cling instead to God. I know this to be true: the only way that we can ever be free from worry is by surrendering it to God and having the faith to trust that He will provide. We don't simply hold God's hands, we *cling* to Him with all that we have.

Perhaps this is the greatest and most important characteristic of a woman. No, that is not saying it strongly enough. This *is* the greatest characteristic of a woman: she must be able to continually surrender her heart, her very self to God, and hold tightly to God with all that she has, all that she is, and all that she will someday become. Only when she surrenders to Him can she laugh at the days to come. It is through surrender that she will be set free of all of her anxiety and find her true worth and dignity in Him. Surrender will lead to lasting peace. By clinging to God she will be able to live out the great commandment described in Scripture, "Therefore, you shall love the Lord, your God, will all your heart, and with all your soul, and with all your strength."[23] Remaining close to God and loving Him with all that she has, the woman of worth will know what it means to be strong, because His strength will flow through her. A deep and personal relationship with God will lead the woman of worth to desire to be clothed. Her relationship with God will move her to be pursued and honored and held to a higher standard, instead of being used and unappreciated. Truly, clinging to God is the most important trait in a woman of worth. It is all too easily forgotten. The woman of worth discovers that when she yields to God's plan for her life she can find joy and laughter in the days before her, and in the days to come. We become far too focused on what we need to *do* as women and we forget about who we should *be.* We should be women who throw ourselves at the foot of the Cross, who abandon ourselves to Him with every breath we take. Only then can we *do* the things that bring Him glory, only then can we be *worthy.*

---

[23] Deuteronomy 6:5.

Fierce

Women are called to be fierce, albeit in an entirely different way than men are. When we are honest with ourselves and God, we realize that the heart of a woman is unquestionably and undeniably fierce. The fierce heart of a woman reflects the fierce heart of God, in much the same way that our modesty, strength, dignity, and laughter do. Think about a mother searching for her kidnapped child, or the woman fighting tooth and nail to put herself through college to better her life. These are women we do not want to cross. In a similar way, God's love is fierce: we wouldn't want to cross Him as He searches for His lost children. We see God's fierce love as He fights for our hearts and desires to lead us to a better life. We are fierce and it is time we stopped hiding the fierceness in our hearts. Denying our fierce and feminine hearts denies the way that God made us, it is insulting, not only to ourselves, but to God as well.

Think of the women you admire most. Isn't there something fierce in their hearts and the way they live their lives, the way they carry themselves? There are a lot of women I admire, but no one I admire more than my own mother. My mom was the first woman to show me what it means to be fierce. Her heart remained strong and beautiful, tender and compassionate, no matter what life threw at us. As I've grown up, she has shown new strength. We faced tough times as a family: both of my parents lost jobs, relatives passed away, and we faced a number of struggles, yet my mother was fierce through all of it. She remained steadfast and constant in her love for my father, and for my brother and me. There is something wildly fierce about the heart of my mother, something I've always admired and strive to imitate each and every day. She isn't rude or abrasive but she defends those she loves and cares about with a fiery, unmatched passion. There are countless stories I could tell about the times she would 'go to bat' for me with teachers in school when she or I felt that I had been wronged. I'd even bet that some of those teachers remember my mother to this day! The women that we admire possess characteristics we want to emulate. Most, if not all of the women I admire, are fierce in their prayer life, fierce in their faith, their defense of the faith, fierce in the way they love their families, or fierce in the way they pursue the heart of God.

Call to mind the female characters you love most in the movies. I love to watch chick-flicks and I can be a sap for a romantic comedy, but of half the time I want to yell at the women in the movies for being so cowardly, and all together spineless. The characters I admire in movies are all intensely fierce women.

The first character that comes to my mind is Lizzy in *Pride & Prejudice*. I've given talks on that movie, led retreats on it, and practically have the whole movie memorized. I've watched it so many times my DVD skips, especially around my favorite scenes, the scenes where Lizzy shines as a gloriously strong woman. Do you know what word I think of when I watch Lizzy? Fierce. She overhears the wealthy and powerful Mr. Darcy say that she is "barely tolerable" and throws it in his face mere minutes later. She doesn't let anyone put her down or make her feel less than worthy of happiness, joy, and love. She forms her opinions and holds to them, however wrong they may end up being (hence the title). The scene in which Mr. Darcy first professes his love for Lizzy is my favorite scene. Lizzy doesn't let Mr. Darcy up for anything. She calls him out on his misconceptions, on his false beliefs, and his hurtful, ungentlemanly words. She is unrelenting in her beliefs, and her desire for true and passionate love. She won't allow herself to be unhappy or to be made to feel small or unworthy. She is a prime example of a fierce woman.

The movie *The Nativity Story* is another wonderful example of what it means to be a fierce woman. Mary, humble though she may be, doesn't let the world get to her. Yes, she is pregnant before she is married and her sin brings great shame upon her and her family. She doesn't give in. She trusts in the Lord's plan unfailingly. She is fierce. The women I admire most are fierce beyond belief because they know who they are and whose they are. They are open-minded and yet unrelenting when it comes to their core beliefs. They are beautiful and strong, and I wouldn't ever be caught dead crossing one of them.

Women of worth are clothed, they are strong, often beyond their own wildest dreams, and they are dignified. Women of worth are also passionate, fierce women and their own fierceness comes from the wild and fierce heart of God Himself. Why deny it any longer?

The Wellsprings of Life

I own a lot of bibles. It comes from being a theology major in college, and a youth minister after that. I own them in different colors and different translations, some are far more well-worn than others, and I use them for different things. In nearly all of my bibles one verse is highlighted, underlined, and starred: Proverbs 4:23. It reads, "With closest custody, guard your heart, for in it are the sources of life." Some translations say that in our hearts are the wellsprings of life. The word wellspring conjures up an image of our hearts as a well that we can draw upon. Sometimes the well runs dry. The wellspring of our hearts is to be, like Saint Bernard of Clairvaux wrote, a reservoir that overflows with God's love. Our wellspring runs dry when we are not allowing God to fill it, when we close our hearts off to Him and His love. But, when we let Him love us, our wellspring is full of life, which is exactly why it needs to be guarded. God resides in our hearts so why would we not guard Him? Surely He is God, He doesn't *need* our protection, but we need to guard Him in our hearts because we need to make sure that we keep Him there, and that He is the most prominent force filling up our wellspring. We find our inner fierceness by taking care of our own hearts and making sure that the well is filled with the Waters of Eternal Life.

Imagine my joy when I found an author who writes about Proverbs 4:23 almost as much as I've read it. John Eldredge expands on the verse as he writes, "Care for your heart. Above all else. Not only for your own sake; not even primarily for your own sake. Do it in order to love better, for the sake of those who need you. And they need you. Remember – this is our most desperate hour."[1] Care for your heart, not just as a simple task on that never ending to do list you've got going, care for your heart *above all else*. As if your life and happiness depend on it, because, let's

---

[1] Eldredge, John. *Waking the Dead: The Glory of a Heart Fully Alive*. Nashville, TN: Thomas Nelson, 2003. 212.

face it, they do. Your heart is what makes you fierce and when we fail to care for it, we cease being the fierce women God is calling us to be. Guard for your heart because God makes His home in our hearts, and you wouldn't want to leave it dirty and dusty for the greatest house guest of all time, would you? Protect your heart because God loves your heart, and because you need your heart. Scripture tells us to care for our hearts because others need us, they need our tender and fierce hearts.

We care for our hearts so that we can love as God loves: beautifully, unconditionally, unreservedly, and fiercely. Saint Peter reminds us that we have been "purified…by obedience to the truth for sincere mutual love" and that we are to "love one another intensely from a [pure] heart."[2] We can't possibly hope to be purified unless we remain close to the Truth, so close in fact, that it lives and moves and has Its being within our hearts. It is Truth, residing in our hearts, that purifies us by continued obedience and makes it possible for sincere mutual love to exist. Resting in His love we can, in turn, love one another from a pure heart. Be aware that we aren't supposed to love each other in a cursory, wishy-washy kind of way. Saint Peter challenges us to love one another as fiercely and intensely as God loves us. We only achieve such love by allowing Love to make His home in us. It is better for our hearts to be a reservoir than for them to be a canal, because a canal can be emptied, but a reservoir always contains God's intense and fierce love.

What happens when the outside world threatens our wellsprings? Our happiness and our hearts are going to be

---

[2] 1 Peter 1:22

challenged and attacked by the Father of Lies. We are called to take an active role in guarding our hearts and remaining strong in Him, no matter what is happening in the world around us. We've seen the stakes, the battle is before us. Scripture tells us to remain awake and sober for the Lord will come like a thief in the dead of night.[3] Our love for others is not an investment on which we can expect, or even necessarily hope for a return, and yet we are called to love others. Blessed Mother Teresa is often credited with saying, "People are unreasonable, illogical, and self-centered. Love them anyway." Love – true love – remains love whether we acknowledge it and accept it or not. Saint John writes, "Whoever does not love remains in death."[4] Plain and simple, to live is to love. To love, as Jesus shows us, is to suffer, but to suffer is to be raised from death and live with Him in unending glory. Jesus tells us, "Remain in my love" because His love is life-giving.[5] Guard your hearts above all else, because they are fiercely needed.

Desperately Needed

Do you ever feel that as worthy as God finds you, you still aren't enough, or you still don't have what it takes to enter into this battle of life and be victorious? Fear not, for even Saint Augustine felt the same way. He wrote, "The house of my soul is too small for You to come to it. May it be enlarged by You. It is in ruins: restore it."[6] Saint Augustine knew that his heart was in ruins from sin, and yet he takes his broken heart to God and asks Him to

---

[3] 2 Peter 3:10, 1 Thessalonians 5:2.
[4] 1 John 3:14.
[5] John 15:9.
[6] Augustine. Trans. Henry Chadwick. *Confessions*. Oxford: Oxford UP, 1991. 6.

restore it. We know our task as worthy women can be overwhelming, which is why this prayer of Saint Augustine is so perfect for us. The house of our heart and soul is too small for Him, it is too small to house and contain enough of His love for our mission in this life.

Come to our hearts, Lord. Ransom them to Yourself. Restore them, heal them and enlarge them so that we may share more of Your love with more of Your children. Enlarge our hearts to love more, and to be more perfectly the worthy women You have created us to be.

Look around and it won't take long to find a man or a woman who doesn't believe in their own worth. Each day people are falling prey to more and more of Satan's lies, and God passionately desires to engage all of His children in this battle. He wants to reveal to His children that He already finds us worthy. Our fierce and wonderfully female hearts are needed. As Stasi Eldredge puts it, "There is something fierce in the heart of a woman. Simply insult her children, her man, or her best friend and you'll get a taste of it. A woman is a warrior too. But she is meant to be a warrior in a uniquely feminine way."[7] We are warriors. We are meant to defend those we love with our protective and maternal natures, whether we have biological offspring of our own or not. This warrior quality about us isn't something we've simply learned or adapted to over time; it is written into our nature because it, like all of our best qualities, reflects the heart of God. Tender and yet fierce, He defends us and protects us more often

---

[7] Eldredge, John, and Stasi Eldredge. *Captivating: Unveiling the Mystery of a Woman's Soul*. Nashville: Nelson, 2005. 11.

than we will ever know. Maybe you won't be like Mulan and cut all your hair off to fight in a great war, but you have a role to play in this battle, a role that is uniquely yours and uniquely feminine. Eldredge continues,

> "Sometime before the sorrows of life did their best to kill it in us, most young women wanted to be a part of something grand, something important. Before doubt and accusation take hold, most little girls sense that they have a vital role to play; they want to believe there is something in them that is needed and needed desperately."[8]

It is time to unleash that little girl inside us that still believes we are needed. The games we played as children, the ones where we wanted to be the damsel who was rescued, the nurse who healed the wounded, or the mother that fed everyone supper, all speak to this primal desire to have a critical role to play. Rid yourself of doubt and accusations and remember the little girl you once were, the one who longed for a vital role to play. The very thing she desired lays before you now, a crucial and critical role to play in the greatest adventure there ever will be: the battle for our souls.

Harsh Realizations

I am broken and flawed, and aren't we all? I'm not always as strong or as fierce as I know God is calling me to be. Thank God that a friend of mine allowed the Lord to speak through her when she told me, "You are stronger than you think you are, so much stronger. You have a strong, fierce heart and I don't know why you don't let it shine. You are a strong woman and I wish you

---

[8] Ibid.

saw yourself that way, because I don't think you see yourself as strong." When I heard those words it was like a sucker punch that knocks the wind out of you so completely that you wonder if you'll ever breathe again. I was overcome with a myriad of emotions upon hearing these words, emotions for my loss of fierceness, for the strength I'd lost, sadness and yet relief that my friend could see through my walls to the depths of my heart. As the tears began to flow, my heart was, at long last, broken open to the healing love of God.

I sat there, stunned, and yet oddly thankful for my friend's words and thought to myself, "Oh, fierce. I had almost nearly forgotten about you. You are the word I keep coming back to in this quest to find my heart again. You are the word that keeps popping up in my meditations, in my readings, and in my heart. You are the word that just won't leave me alone." I probably would have been a lot better off had my friend said that whole statement without using the word fierce. This conversation about my heart, where it was or wasn't, is an on-going conversation between God and me. Throughout the conversation with my friend I kept coming back to my desire to be fierce. I used to feel fierce, there was a time I felt unbroken because I knew I was whole in Him. Sometimes we buy into Satan's lies and fall back into those old coffins. Sometimes we try to love someone or something else as though they are our God. Saint Catherine of Siena said that everything short of God must and will disappoint us. All too often we don't realize that we are trying to make someone or something else into our God. We lose our fierceness because we don't let God fill our wellspring. Sure, we may let Him put some water in our well, but we don't let Him fill it completely with His abundant love. Instead, we try to fill our wellsprings will designer clothes, nights out on the town, or any number of things the world tries to sell us. We fear letting God will our wellspring because then He might ask us to follow Him into uncharted territory.

Perhaps we lose our fierce hearts because we let fear overwhelm us, fear of the unknown, fear of the future, fear of uncertainty, fear of being happy, and fear of fear itself. There are perhaps a million different reasons why we lose our fierce hearts, all I know is that somewhere in this battle of life I lost that fierceness, that wholeness, and not only did I not know where I'd lost it, I didn't know how to get it back.

After hearing those words from my friend, I spent a lot of time reflecting on strong women and women I admire for the fire they have in their hearts, a fire I so desperately wanted to burn brightly in my own heart again. I thought if I could find a few examples, surely I would know how to get my fiercely feminine heart back. All I could come up with was Mary in *The Nativity Story* and Lizzy in *Pride & Prejudice*. Both are wonderful examples and yet they just didn't seem to be enough. When it comes down to it we don't know much about Mary. She is strong and fierce to be sure, and yet I've always felt that understanding and relating to her fierce heart is just beyond my reach. We have these two great women who embody what it means to be fierce. So what? They aren't enough. I want more concrete examples of women I can relate to and imitate in my own quest for fierceness. These two women are great examples but they don't get at what it means to *be* fierce. They get at what you *do* to be fierce. These women didn't back down, they held their heads high, they knew what they believed in and they stuck to it. These are women to be adored, sought after, and yet they are women to be feared if you ever dared to cross them. I don't want a painfully lengthy list of things I need to *do* to be fierce or to be deemed worthy, I want to know about the heart of such a woman. What is it in the heart of a woman that makes her fierce? So I took my questions to God in prayer:

"What does it mean to be fierce?
What does it mean to be fierce *as a woman?*

Lord, show me that I am strong. Show me that I am fierce. Help me to see myself as You see me. I trust that You see something in me that I all too often fail to see, and fail to live out, and isn't that the truth with so many of Your daughters and Your sons? I am challenged, then, in these times to walk by faith. If Truth were a light at the end of a dark tunnel, I fear I would fail to see it even then. But my heart must be more than something You see, make my strength and fierceness known to me in the depths of my soul. As it stands now, the truth that I do have a fierce heart has been swallowed by a hurricane of lies. This ship was made to float, to sail, and to conquer the storms of the oceans, to traverse the mighty seas. This ship was made for glory, and not just for any glory but for Your glory.

Lord,
What does it mean to be fierce?
What does it mean to be a *fierce woman?"*

The answer that kept coming back to my heart is that we must stop being chickens. There are times in life that we want to say something, speak up, challenge those we love, encourage them to be better, holier versions of themselves. All too often we remain silent. On the off chance that we do speak up, what ends up coming out is some watered down, highly diluted, overly fluffy version of what we really want to say. I'd equate it with throwing cotton balls at people, as if cotton balls will even get their attention, much less spur them on to holiness. There was a moment of grace when my friend let the Lord speak the words that broke down the walls in my heart. Those words broke me down like an egg in a tornado - I didn't stand a chance, but broken eggs make great scrambled eggs. All is not yet lost.

That moment of grace, painful though it may have been, couldn't have happened if my friend hadn't first opened her own heart to God. My friend knew that the words needed to come out and as soon as they were out in the open we both knew they were God's words, meant just for my heart. Still, had fear crippled her, I may never have had this revelation. All of those times we've thought about saying something to one of our friends, challenging them and we've bitten our tongue, have we been keeping, perhaps even stopping, potential moments of grace, growth, and revelation from happening for them?

Being fierce, and being fierce *as a woman*, must be more than a lack of chicken-ness. Fierce and fear, they sound so similar and yet they are so far apart. To be a fierce woman one must not be overcome by fear – in other words don't throw proverbial cotton balls at your friends – but she must also open her heart to God's heart, above and beyond anything and anyone else. First and foremost. Eternally and perpetually. I could say it a thousand different ways and I feel as though I must because we forget that our hearts are ransomed to God, always. Not just until some shiny new toy shows up, not just until we think we've attained happiness on our own, not until some knight in shining armor shows up, but always and forever our hearts must reside in the depths of His. She, this revered woman of worth, must let God's fierce, loving ways flow through *everything* she.

Moments of grace, growth, hope, love, healing, peace, and revelation are on the line. Our hearts and souls are on the line. Our ticket into Heaven is on the line. This is no time for playing games, or for shrinking behind our masks of fear and insecurity. The world needs our fierce *feminine* hearts. The world needs the fierce love of God to be spoken through hearts full, not of fear, but of fierce and unquenchable love. He is fierce, mighty, and majestic to behold; may our hearts be fierce, mighty, majestic, and even inspiring to behold, and may He speak through our hearts to heal and restore others to Truth.

You Are Needed.

Consider it an ad for the perfect job. I once heard Mark Hall, the lead singer of Casting Crowns, give his testimony, and in it he tells how he realized that God didn't need him. It sounds wildly depressing, right? God doesn't need you. He is God, He has no need for anything at all. However, the God of the Universe, the Father, the great I AM, desperately and passionately *wants **you*** and happens to think that you are the perfect candidate for a specific role in the history of salvation. He has no need for anything and yet He still wants, longs, and waits for you, just as you are.

Paul writes to the Ephesians, charging them, "Therefore, it says: "Awake, O sleeper, and arise from the dead, and Christ will give you light."[9] It is time to be awakened. God has awakened your heart to the truth and the beauty that you are worthy and loved, and that He created you to be His beloved. He finds you worthy, worthy of love, of life, and even worth dying for. Therefore Paul encourages and challenges us, "Watch carefully then how you live, not as foolish persons but as wise, making the most of the opportunity, because the days are evil. Therefore, do not continue in ignorance, but try to understand what is the will of the Lord."[10] You can deny your worthiness all you want, but you can no longer continue in complete ignorance of it. Try to understand what the will of the Lord is, because the days before us are fraught with the sinister plots of Satan. God wants you to let your light shine. He wants you to expose the lies of Satan. Allow God to put you on a lampstand; open your heart to being worthy and to being found worthy by the God of the Universe.

The journey of allowing God to free you from your coffins is a long one. The journey of being found worthy can be just as treacherous, even though Christ has already won the battle for our hearts. Living life as a woman of worth is by no means a walk in the park. Jesus tells us, "In the world you will have trouble."[11] Plain

---

[9] Ephesians 5:14
[10] Ephesians 5:15-17.

and simple, we are going to struggle and suffer, but He restores us in hope as He invites us, "take courage, I have conquered the world."[12] Jesus has overcome, let us rest our hearts in the knowledge that He is fierce, and He has conquered all the evils in the world. Our journey is not yet over. We are moving towards holiness, perfection, and the Heart that bled for love us. We are bound for Heaven. Paul again exhorts us as he writes, "conduct yourselves as worthy of the God who calls you into his kingdom and glory."[13] We believe that, by His grace, we are worthy; the challenge now is to conduct ourselves accordingly.

Saint Paul, filled with the wisdom of the Spirit, wrote a beautiful prayer to the church in Philippi. His prayer for them is my prayer for you as we let the weight of God's love, and the knowledge that He finds us worthy, drench our souls. "And this is my prayer: that your love may increase ever more and more in knowledge and every kind of perception, to discern what is of value, so that you may be pure and blameless for the day of Christ, filled with the fruit of righteousness that comes through Jesus Christ for the glory and praise of God."[14] Amen.

---

[11] John 16:33.

[12] Ibid.

[13] 1 Thessalonians 2:12.

[14] Philippians 1:9-11.

Acknowledgments

There is simply no way that this book would have ever been possible without the love, encouragement, and support of more people than I can ever list here. In some way, every person I've ever met has had an influence on who I am and, therefore, on this book. Thank you to every person who has touched my life, my heart, and my soul.

Words can never express how truly grateful I am for my wonderful readers, both of this book and of my blog. Your prayers and support got me through more late nights and spiritual battles than you may ever know; I'm blessed by you every single day. Rest assured that you remain in my prayers. To all of my friends far and wide, literally spanning the globe, who previewed the book and gave me invaluable feedback, this book wouldn't be what it is without your guidance. I am, from the very depths of my heart, grateful to all those that helped me with editing and wisdom, especially Liesl, Theresa, Julie, Derek, Anne, Aunt Suzy, and Grandma Karen, this book is stronger, flows better, and makes more sense because of you. Thank you to my incredible brother who sat with me and helped me format the book, no matter how annoyed I got at the whole process. Who could forget my wonderful parents? I'm eternally grateful for your unfailing love and support, not only as I wrote and edited this book, but from the very moment I became your daughter to today.

Finally, thank you to the God who loves me into existence, who breathes life into my heart and soul, and moves me in more ways than I can ever put words to. You are the reason for everything I do. May this book bring You glory.